ANTI-RACIST PROBATION PRACTICE

DEDICATION

To all black and white people who are working together to end racism and to all those who are on the receiving end of racism because it is not being addressed.

Anti-racist
Probation Practice

Lena Dominelli   Lennie Jeffers
Graham Jones   Sakhile Sibanda
Brian Williams

arena

Published by
Arena
Ashgate Publishing Limited
Gower House
Croft Road
Aldershot
Hants GU11 3HR
England

Ashgate Publishing Company
Old Post Road
Brookfield
Vermont 05036
USA

British Library Cataloguing in Publication Data

Dominelli, Lena
  Anti-racist Probation
  Practice
  I. Title
  364.630941

Library of Congress Catalog Card Number: 95–78940

ISBN 1 85742 280 5 (paperback)
ISBN 1 85742 328 3 (hardback)

Typeset in 10pt Palatino by Raven Typesetters, Chester.
Printed in Great Britain by Hartnolls Ltd., Bodmin

Contents

A note on the authors

Lena Dominelli holds the Chair in Social Administration at the University of Sheffield. She is author of various books, including: *Women in Focus: Female Offenders and Community Service Orders* (1983); *Love and Wages* (1986); *Anti-Racist Social Work* (1988); *Feminist Social Work* (1989) (with E McLeod); *Women and Community Action* (1990); *Women Across Continents: Feminist Comparative Social Policy* (1991); *Gender, Sex Offenders and Probation Practice* (1991); and *'Contaminating Knowledge': Sociological Social Work* (forthcoming). In addition to being a teacher, author and researcher, she has worked as a community worker, probation officer and social worker.

Lennie Jeffers was born in the West Indies and came to live in the UK at the age of 6. He grew up in Cleckheaton, a small town in the industrial West Riding of Yorkshire, until he moved away to London in pursuit of higher education in 1978. He started as a volunteer with the Probation Service in Leeds in 1982, and has worked as a qualified probation officer in that city since 1986. He has always had a strong interest and commitment to anti-racism and justice. In 1987, he co-edited the West Yorkshire Probation Service Branch of NAPO's booklet, *Racism and Probation*. He has also taught social work students at the University of Sheffield.

Graham Jones completed his social work studies at the University of Sheffield and went on to work for the South Yorkshire Probation Service, where he developed his interests in anti-racist social work, focusing primarily on addressing the issues of working in anti-racist ways with both black and white workers and 'clients'. Prior to this, he had been actively involved in anti-racist initiatives in London.

Sakhile Sibanda has had a varied life experience. Born in a British colony, she was involved in the liberation struggle from colonial rule in Zimbabwe from the age of 17. She has worked as a fund-raiser and administrator with a national charity in Zimbabwe. She has also been involved with a community programme for the long-term unemployed in the UK. She has worked as a probation officer with the South Yorkshire Probation Service which also seconded her to become a practice teacher and Practice Teaching Development Worker for the South Yorkshire Diploma in Social Work Programme. She is currently lecturing at the University of Sheffield and is Co-director of the Practice Teaching Evaluation Project there.

Brian Williams is currently teaching at the University of Keele. He has held a joint post as Lecturer at Sheffield University and probation officer with the South Yorkshire Probation Service. His previous posts included Lecturer in Social Work at Teesside Polytechnic and probation officer for the Warwickshire Probation Service and Durham Probation Service. He has a number of publications, which include the following: 'Caring Professionals or Street-Level Bureaucrats? The Case of Probation Officers' Work with Prisoners' in *Howard Journal of Criminal Justice* (November 1992); *Work with Prisoners* (1991); *Bail Information Schemes* (1992); *Probation Values* (1995); and *The Probation Service and Victims of Crime* (with Mike Kosh, 1995).

Acknowledgements

Many people have helped us with this book, and not all of them can be named. We would like to thank everyone who helped us to develop the initial idea. In particular, we would like to mention Mary Mustoe, Jane Watt and Gini Whitehead. We are also indebted to everyone who took the trouble to discuss our ideas with us while we were writing it. These include: Barbara Godfrey, Steve Johnson, Cordell Pillay, Annette Thomstone and all those who helped with the research for Chapter 5. Their contribution has been enormous.

The way in which we chose to write the book as a collective venture was time-consuming but rewarding. We have learnt a great deal from each other in the process. Our experience together has been a stimulating and valuable one, and it will feel strange when we stop meeting to discuss drafts and deadlines. We all owe a great deal to Sue Baldock in the Department of Sociological Studies at Sheffield University for her secretarial support and the patient and efficient way in which she has co-ordinated the massive amount of paperwork involved in the project.

We would each like to thank our institutions and colleagues for making it possible for us to get on with our task. We are also grateful to our colleagues, and to the students we work with, for the stimulus and the case materials they have provided.

Finally, we thank our families for tolerating our absences and supporting us in the writing of the book. Many thanks are due to: Nicholas and David; Joan, Helen and Nathan; Jill, Lily and Stephen; Musa; and Sue and Jess.

Lena, Lennie, Graham, Sakhile and Brian
Sheffield
October 1995

Introduction

'Race', racism and anti-racism continue to be highly emotive and controversial topics, notwithstanding the attempts that black and white people have made in establishing more egalitarian social relationships in social work.[1] Despite the promulgation of anti-racist or equal opportunities policies, neither the criminal justice system in general nor the Probation Service in particular have been immune from charges of their perpetuating racism in the course of administering justice; heated debates about what ought to be done to eradicate racism from their midst, and lamentations about the slow progress in responding to these criticisms. We believe this issue will not go away of its own accord. Nor will racism disappear if there isn't a full understanding of what is happening and what needs to be done to realise anti-racist practice at *all levels* of the criminal justice system and including all of its agencies such as the Probation Service.

Despite the space limitations of this book, we intend to provide an analysis of what is going wrong in the Probation Service and make concrete suggestions for improving practice in anti-racist directions. Although we concentrate on the Probation Service as one element of the criminal justice system, we think that the analysis and ways of moving forward that we propose offer models which can, with the appropriate modifications, be emulated in other parts of the criminal justice system. We feel that this book is timely because anti-racist social work is under attack from the highest political levels. At the bleakest moments of despair, it is important that there remain rays of hope in moving forward on this front. We hope that our book, with its proposals for improving current practice, will play a role in this regard. Certainly, we have found that writing this book together has been an important source of optimistic hope when many of our colleagues have been gloomy about the prospects of safeguarding anti-racist social work.

We chose to write this book collectively, despite our different experiences, because we felt it was important to show that black and white people could work sensitively with each other and promote egalitarian relationships amongst ourselves. The group was made up of one black woman, one black man, two white men and one white woman. The supportive nature of the group also meant that we could welcome one of the white male authors into our midst when we had already begun writing the text. We would recommend this way of proceeding to others who wish to work in anti-racist ways.

The structure of the book

This book will evaluate the extent to which the Probation Service as part of the criminal justice system operating within a variety of settings – the court, the field, day-centres, hostels and prisons – has taken on board holistic change which involves both grassroots personnel and managers working together in anti-racist directions. It will also examine the extent to which change in the criminal justice system more generally is necessary for advancement in anti-racist directions in a specific part of it, such as the Probation Service. It will also compare initiatives – for example, training – as a vehicle for developing anti-racist practice in the criminal justice system.

The 'unpacking' of the dynamics of racism (and the other forms of oppression which interact with it) will include a consideration of form and process at the following levels, which will provide the common framework or themes which will link the different chapters in the book together. These are:

- 'client'–worker relationships;
- worker–worker relationships;
- employee–employer relationships.[2]

With regard to 'client'–worker interaction, the focus will be on the work probation workers undertake in developing relationships with their 'clients', whether they are writing a Pre-Sentence Report (PSR), running offence-focused groups; referring 'clients' to other parts of the service (for example, probation centres, hostels, voluntary groups and psychiatric support services); supervising offenders in the community; providing throughcare, or undertaking court work. The dynamics and processes which are involved in developing anti-racist practice will be examined through case study materials which the authors themselves have amassed in the course of their work with 'clients'.

The worker–worker relationship will be examined as part of the process of working with others to further the aims and objectives of the Probation Service. Black probation workers' routine experience of racism from both 'clients' and workers requires survival strategies which address both personal and organisational levels of interaction. These strategies will be considered in light of the responses which both white and black probation workers need to undertake to promote anti-racist practice. Monitoring mechanisms, gatekeeping systems and resource allocation policies will also be examined in terms of their ability to provide the safeguards claimed of them.

Employer–employee relations are crucial in setting the parameters within which organisational change occurs. The policies that Probation Services operating as employers are prepared to endorse and the resources allocated to their realisation are critical in establishing an organisational climate supportive of anti-racist initiatives, and give managers a vital role in fostering anti-racist perspectives. The employers' practices *vis-à-vis* supervision of main grade officers, promotion procedures, training provisions and management styles are crucial in fostering upward mobility by black probation officers. Important managerial concerns which, if mishandled, can exacerbate racial divisions rather than eliminate them include the following: employers' approaches to addressing the conflicts that anti-racist initiatives can set up between black and white probation staff/workers; employers' handling of a potential backlash resting on the erroneous premise that those black officers who have 'made it in the system' are 'not up to it', and employers' dismantling of the obstacles introduced by probation staff/workers who resent the specific questions anti-racist perspectives pose about their work. We will use case study materials to examine these issues in depth later in the book.

Thus both service delivery and the management of equal opportunities within the Probation Service will be encompassed in our remit. In other words, this book attempts to take a *holistic view* of probation within society according to its roles and functions as an institution within the criminal justice system.

Chapter 1 examines the dynamics of racism as they operate in the Probation Service and sets these within the context of the criminal justice system more broadly. It considers the question of why, despite the promulgation of 'equal opportunities policies' across the country and the pressures to change the Probation Service applied by black activists, anti-racist lobbyists within the National Association of Probation Officers (NAPO), the Association of Black Probation Officers (ABPO), the National Association of Asian Probation Staff (NAAPS) and other anti-racists, the picture for black and white women and black men interacting with the criminal justice system is as depressing as ever. Justice is being denied to black women and men in the work environment, and to black 'clients' in the dispensation of justice itself.

Chapter 2 traces these issues as they impinge on both educational processes and employment practices. It traces these across black probation officers' experience of surviving racism both in educational establishments and in the Probation Service as officers going through the confirmation process as they establish themselves as qualified practitioners, and draws out those forces and lessons which have broader relevance.

Chapter 3 examines the daily struggles against racism undertaken by black people. It draws heavily on the strategies developed by black proba- tion officers as they supervise 'clients', write Pre-Sentence Reports, liaise with colleagues and engage with other institutions in the welfare and criminal justice systems in the course of their work, and generalises from these.

Chapter 4 considers the importance of training in working on white proba- tion workers' own racism and anti-racist struggles. All too often, anti-racist practice for white people has been defined as what white people do for black people – improve services, recruit black people to the profession – thereby casting black people in a passive light and negating black people's struggles against being patronised in these ways. Training should also cover what work white people need to do as white people with white people: for example, building support networks to keep up their morale when engaging in anti-racist organisational change; providing training aimed at their needs as white people trying to become anti-racists, and developing their under- standing of racist dynamics at the subtle levels of operation.

Chapter 5 looks at black people's experiences of the prison system. This is a much neglected area of research, but this chapter highlights the specifics of oppression in this setting and examines the resistance black people have developed in fighting oppression and adapting to the realities of imprison- ment as they encounter them.

Chapter 6 presents the concluding remarks, identifying guidelines for good practice in the process. These will indicate how anti-racist practice encompasses other social divisions and takes on board the needs of both black and white people so that we can work together in egalitarian partner- ships to eradicate racism.

Notes

1   'Race' is used in quotes to denote that the term is being used as a socially-created construct – which requires the politicisation of a physical phenology to indicate that one phenological type is superior to another – not a biologically-determined one.
2   Quotation marks are used around the word 'client' to indicate the problematic nature of the term and the controversy surrounding its use.

1 More than injustice

Justice is the currency which is expected to circulate throughout the criminal justice system, and in most people's view, that system is the institution which is entrusted with the duty of ensuring that justice is both done and seen to be done. However, when evidence to the contrary occasionally comes to light, as has happened in the long, drawn-out attempts to get at the 'truth' in recent well-publicised cases of miscarriages of justice, such as the Guildford Six, the Maguires, the Birmingham Four, the Bradford Twelve and the Cardiff Four, it is hotly disputed (Kennedy, 1992). If errors are admitted, they are usually attributed to a few corrupt individuals rather than being considered signs of failure in the system itself.

That the problems of the criminal justice system (CJS) result from more than the traits of unreliable or incompetent individuals is evident if we examine its structures as well as its personnel. Such an examination reveals that the decision-making processes, regardless of whether these concern policy, legislation or practice in the CJS, lie primarily in the hands of white middle- and upper-class men (King and May, 1985). A wide range of people – particularly if they are working-class, women or black – are excluded from these. Yet it is mainly working-class people, black people and women who are disproportionately represented amongst those at the receiving end of its deliberations as alleged offenders.

We use the term 'black people' to mean people who are oppressed or excluded from holding socio-economic power and being involved in society's decision-making structures because they are considered 'black', regardless of their actual skin colour; in the UK this includes people of Asian and African descent. Our use of this category does not suggest that the people encompassed by it are a homogeneous group. Indeed, we recognise that they are heterogeneous peoples with differing origins, languages, religions, and cultural and historical traditions. They are more unlike each other than they are like each other. But what they have in common is their

1

experience of racism – their exclusion from the public domain on the grounds of an assumed phenology of 'race' and racial types.

The exclusion of a wide spectrum of people from the decision-making apparatus within the CJS, coupled with the over-representation of society's marginalised groups as the objects of its ministrations, is a main preoccupation of this book. However, the CJS is a vast institution which cannot be covered in the confines of one short text. Hence we will focus on one section of it – the Probation Service, which presents in microcosm the issues which challenge the CJS more generally.

By examining specific areas of probation practice (from Pre-Sentence Reports to throughcare), and by considering both qualifying and in-service training, we will show how racism operates and how anti-racist practice can be achieved.

The decision-makers

Mirroring the society of which it is a part, the Probation Service is riven by social divisions. Crucial decisions about its resourcing and development lie in the hands of the Home Secretary who, to this point in UK history, has always been a white male. Within the institution itself, the major decision-makers are white men. White women make up only 8 per cent of the Chief Probation Officer grade, and no black person has made it to this level thus far. Moreover, although both white women and black people are now coming into the profession in greater numbers, they are still located primarily at the main grade and lower levels. White women now form 45 per cent of the main grade officers, and in the last four or five years have been drawn increasingly into the ranks of middle management as Senior Probation Officers (NACRO, 1992).

It is still unclear whether this progress is the result of changes in employment policies arising from pressure women have placed on the Service, or whether it is part of a broader structural process, namely the feminisation of the Probation Service. If it is part of the latter, it is a sign of the decrease in status and reduced professional clout which the Probation Service is undergoing rather than indicating a gain for women (Dominelli, 1995). Yet even this marginal improvement in the position of women is precarious. In early 1995, the Home Secretary expressed concern at the increasing numbers of married women joining the Probation Service and threatened to turn it into a uniformed 'Corrections Service' staffed with former army personnel and police officers.

Black people are present to a lesser extent, in that only 3 per cent of the workforce is made up of black people, and these are more likely to be found at the lower levels including those of main grade officer, Probation Service

Officer (a reclassification of the previous Probation Service Assistant) and volunteers (NACRO, 1992). The experiences of black people in their encounters with the system are a major theme of this book.

When it comes to service delivery, neither white women nor black people receive services which are specifically geared to their needs. The Probation Service is awash with stereotypes about womanhood (black and white) and black people which provide the driving force behind the provisions which are made available to them. As a result, services are developed primarily to cater for white male offenders, whilst white women and black people are expected to put up with variants of these. White women are disproportionately represented in custodial settings and are related to as 'sick, mad or bad' (Worrall, 1990; Morris, 1987; Dominelli, 1983). Black people are also disproportionately represented in custodial settings (Hudson, 1990; Sivanandan, 1992). Moreover, the dominant themes which are brought into play regarding them are 'dangerousness' and 'pathology' (Dominelli, 1988; Hall et al., 1978). The 'dangerousness' motif is particularly evident in relation to black women (Dominelli, 1983). These themes are articulated in myriad ways to weave the fabric of racism which threads its way through the criminal justice system as a whole.

Definition of terms

Racism

Racism was defined by Audre Lorde as 'the belief in the inherent superiority of one race over another and thereby the right to dominate' (Lorde, 1984, p. 115). Such beliefs are extended into the public arena and given legitimacy through legislation, policies, cultural norms and behaviours. Thus we can speak of racism as a complex web of interwoven relationships aimed at controlling black people and subordinating their needs to those of the dominant white group. Racism operates at a number of different levels which interact with and build on each other. These are:

- personal racism;
- institutional racism;
- cultural racism (Dominelli, 1988; Bromley and Longino, 1972).

Personal racism concerns the attitudes, beliefs and prejudices against black people held by individuals who aim to put black people down at every opportunity whilst enhancing their own sense of worth and importance. It relies on the presence of the other forms of racism in order to be affirmed in the public arena. But the existence of personal racism is also crucial in maintaining both institutional and cultural racism.

Institutional racism is made up of the routine policies and practices which exclude black people from participating in the decision-making processes of society, enjoying citizenship rights and receiving their share of society's resources. The impact of institutional racism can be either direct or indirect, depending on whether or not black people are deliberately excluded from the system. It relies on the existence of both personal and cultural racism to be maintained and reproduced, and it contributes in turn to the maintenance and reproduction of the other two.

Cultural racism consists of those socially accepted values and norms which ascribe an inferior status to black people and devalue the contribution which they have made to society. It underpins both personal and institutional racism and relies on them for its continuation.

The interconnectedness of these three forms of racism makes it difficult to deal with racism, and suggests that we cannot abolish racism without tackling the problem at all three levels. We will focus on the issues which addressing racism presents in the context of working in the Probation Service from both anti-racist and black perspectives in subsequent chapters of this book. In the course of doing so, we will also provide examples of good practice in working with both black and white people from anti-racist and black perspectives.

Black perspective

Our definition of black perspectives stems from an understanding of how living in a racist society shapes black people's experience as *black* people. In other words, a *black perspective* is about developing a world view which is informed by a person's experience of racial oppression, their desire to comprehend and articulate that experience, and their wish to eradicate the social relations which give rise to racism. Therefore not all black people hold a black perspective. Only those who acknowledge the presence of racism and consider it a political issue which must be tackled for the liberation of black people would be included in our definition of it. A black perspective's commitment to eradicating racism and improving social relations for all people makes it relevant to white people too (see hooks, 1992, 1993).

White perspective

A *white perspective*, on the other hand, is about a world view which takes for granted the existence of racial oppression and does not seek to address the issue of its elimination. Its form varies over time with the changing forms racism assumes. At this historical conjuncture, it concerns itself primarily with redefining racist discourse around culture and ethnicity, as can be evidenced in the discourse of the New Right (see Barker, 1981). Nor does a white perspective acknowledge the enormous advantages which accrue to white people as a result of the existence of racism. In short, a white perspective is another name for a racist perspective, although it need not be this. It is our hope that white people will be able to reclaim a white perspective for more progressive purposes as part of our collective struggle to remove racism from the social agenda.

We do not, therefore, use the term 'white perspective' to signify an anti-racist perspective held by white people. Our reasons for this are the following: white perspectives have historically been racist perspectives, thus the concept for us does not signify a commitment to eliminating racism. Moreover, we are concerned that white people have used the term to denote white supremacy – that is, that whiteness becomes the norm whereby everything is judged (see hooks, 1992, 1993; Ahmad, 1993), and, in the course of exercising that prerogative, white people become less sensitive to what constitutes racial abuse.

Anti-racist perspective

An *anti-racist perspective* takes racism as a fundamental feature of social relations and aims to change these in favour of non-racist, egalitarian ones. Social change is very much a key concern of anti-racists. Anti-racist perspectives provide white people with the tools for transcending racist discourse and enabling them to work with black people who are also working to eliminate racism from social relations from a black perspective (Dominelli, 1988; hooks, 1992, 1993). At this point, a white perspective can be reclaimed by white anti-racist workers attempting to move it away from its racist connotations. We use the term 'anti-racist perspectives' to refer to the views of white people and black people wishing to end racial oppression.

Oppression

Whilst we focus on understanding racism and developing anti-racist alternatives in this book, we do not consider racism as the only form of oppression which the Probation Service needs to address. There are many other forms of oppression which are encountered in our work. These include sexism, homophobia, ageism, disablism, adultism and mentalism, just to name a few. These also feed into and out of each other, making our work even more difficult in the process. Indeed, the complexity of oppression and the interaction between one form of oppression and another make it unlikely that we can deal with one element of it without touching on the others. So, working from anti-racist and black perspectives means that we should be sensitive to other social divisions and take them on board as we proceed with our work.

Working on getting rid of racism can only be a starting point, from which good practice in general must flow. The development of good probation practice is a matter of concern to practitioners, policy-makers and academics. Hence, we would argue it is the concern of *everyone* working in the Probation Service – from the Chief Probation Officer to the Community Service Officer and the receptionist. Moreover, it is the responsibility of all those working in the courts, whether paid or not, and those politically responsible for the criminal justice system.

We define *oppression* as the systematic exclusion of people from the public domain by denying them:

- access to full citizenship rights;
- participation in society's decision-making structures;
- access to socio-economic and political power;
- access to resources;
- the value of their contribution to society.

Oppression, therefore, proceeds on a number of different dimensions, several of which can be present simultaneously. Moreover, we would argue that because it is difficult to separate out these different social dimensions of oppression (except for the purposes of logical argument and the construction of 'ideal types'), we should resist the temptation to order them according to criteria which place them on a hierarchy which pits attending to one social division against doing so for another.

Anti-discriminatory practice

Anti-discriminatory practice deals with only a small portion of the oppressive realities encountered by oppressed people. Its political and moral philosophy is derived from a liberalism which focuses on individual action and piecemeal engineering within a social system which is seen as problematic rather than irredeemable, thereby masking its more repressive elements. Anti-discriminatory approaches to social work concern themselves with access to services – procedures and entitlements, individual action on behalf of or taken directly by those experiencing discrimination – and with the more superficial concerns about language (for example, what someone or something should be called), rather than engaging with the social relations signifying inferiority embedded within language itself. Thus we get anti-discriminatory practice which can go through the hoops of gatekeeping in the Probation Service to eliminate racist and sexist bias, and discover that, none the less, these biases prevail. The following extracts from a Pre-Sentence Report on a black woman which had been cleared as an example of good practice by the gatekeeping system demonstrate our point. The first extract is given under the section on 'current offences':

> Leroi is only the father of one of Gloria's two children. Leroi is a heroin addict and used to spend most of the family income on drugs which caused some conflict and explains Gloria's past involvement in prostitution . . . Gloria tells me she had spent money he needed for his heroin on food. She was also in the company of a male neighbour when Leroi came home, and accepts that the combination of the two factors probably provoked the attack.

The negative stereotypes of Gloria as a woman and as a black woman are abundantly clear. She is presented as a passive victim whose main concern should have been to play the 'proper' wifely role. The contextualising scene is also one which fosters the racist stereotypes of black people as 'dangerous' and irresponsible members of society who are always caught up in drugs and violence. This view is exacerbated by the additional material provided as 'relevant information about the offender':

> Gloria's parents came to England from Jamaica in the 1950s. She comes from a large family, many of whom have been before the courts.

Besides stigmatising Gloria, the above statements feed into stereotypes which problematise black families, and by implication, all black communities.

The complexity of oppression and the interconnectedness of the different forms of racism mean that the struggle to overcome them is difficult and must cover a range of different factors. Some items may be dealt with by an individual operating on his or her own. However, the struggle is likely to necessitate the formation of alliances and organisations which can co-ordinate and carry out activities aimed at eliminating inequalities and re-organising our social relations from an anti-oppressive perspective on a broader front. In this case it would have to include the courts as well as the Probation Service.

Equal opportunities

Policies of *equal opportunities* also limit themselves to a small segment of the framework of oppression. Equal opportunities policies, like those on anti-discriminatory practice, confine themselves largely to access issues – access to the job market and access to services, again very much on an individual-istic basis. The preoccupation is with the number of black people at work, or using a particular service – a matter of quantity, not quality. The need to examine the quality of the services on offer, who defines them as appropriate, who is *really* paying for them and the need to consider the nature of the working relations and working conditions within the workplace are mainly ignored.

An example of the focus on quantity rather than on both quantitative and qualitative aspects of social relations is the following piece of 'equal opportunities' practice:

> A Probation Service instituted an equal opportunities policy and was delighted with the successful response of black people to its advertisements placed in the black and ethnic press. As a result of a recent round of job interviews, 12 per cent of its posts went to black officers. The senior managers who initiated this policy initiative felt pleased with their efforts and deemed these a 'successful outcome to their policy'. The black officers took up their posts and discovered that on top of the normal caseload which was carried by other (white) officers, they were expected to act as the 'race' experts in the office, train their white colleagues on matters of 'race' and racism and take up all issues raised by black 'clients'.

In other words, whilst focusing on quantity – that is, recruiting a significant number of black professionals – the service, through its managers, had neglected to consider the qualitative issues around the working relations and conditions to which black officers would be subjected. As a result, the black probation officers they had employed were being further exploited by the organisation and its personnel in the name of 'making things better'. Racism was being further reinforced when the intention was the opposite.

Thus, for anti-oppressive practice to occur in accordance with anti-racist principles, change has to take place simultaneously on a number of levels – the personal, the institutional and the cultural. Probation officers have to familiarise themselves with a variety of points at which they can exercise leverage and become aware of the range of instruments and personnel on which they can draw in shifting organisational policies and practice away from its anglocentric base. For example, the UK has legislation such as the Race Relations Act 1976, which prohibits discrimination on the basis of 'race' or ethnicity, and which can be used to initiate changes in agency policy and practice. In addition, the requirements of Section 95 of the Criminal Justice Act 1991 impose duties to monitor the impact of racial discrimination within the Probation Service and the criminal justice system more generally.

On the organisational level, the National Association of Probation Officers (NAPO) has developed extensive guidelines addressing a number of different forms of oppression, which can be used to develop more sensitive forms of practice. The Association of Black Probation Officers (ABPO) has addressed a range of issues in probation practice from a black perspective and can provide speakers and activities through which these can be disseminated. The National Association of Asian Probation Staff (NAAPS) has raised the issue of the specific needs of Asian workers. There are other campaigns and networks – for example, the Campaign Against Double

Punishment (CADP), which deals with the deportation of prisoners, opposes deportations and draws attention to the role of the criminal justice system in criminalising law-abiding black people. It has also amassed information about the different forms that bad practice can take and created guidelines for better practice which are of relevance to probation officers working with black people who do not hold UK nationality.

Pressure can be brought to bear on local management at all levels and training officers to ensure that: local communities are involved in the formation of service plans and proposals; services which are provided are more in keeping with anti-racist practice; white probation officers feel more confident in addressing issues of racism, whether they are working with black 'clients' and workers or with white 'clients' and workers, and black staff can work in conditions which are amenable to their full participation in the work of the service.

The task of creating anti-racist probation practice is one for all members of the service, regardless of their rank or status or skin colour.

The Probation Service within the criminal justice system

The Probation Service is part of the criminal justice system. Probation officers are considered officers of the courts. The Probation Service's concern to enforce respectability can often conflict with probation's social work value base which aims to facilitate individuals acquiring more control over their lives and which may judge certain types of 'criminal behaviour' as condonable if not acceptable, for example, prostitution as a way of earning a living (although soliciting rather than prostitution is the actual offence) (see McLeod, 1982). Alongside probation officers, other workers are given the tasks of controlling offenders, monitoring their behaviour and assisting them in leading more socially acceptable lives, for example, Probation Service Officers (previously Probation Service Assistants), Community Service Officers, residential workers in hostels and workers in day-centres. These workers are expected to control offenders – often without receiving adequate preparatory training, particularly in working with black people – despite facing the difficult issues raised by racism daily.

The tension between care and control in the Probation Service and the criminal justice system more generally is one which enables oppression to be replicated by its own policies and practices. Racism, as a form of oppression, is also part of a control structure. First, it rations resources by excluding black people from entitlement; second, it provides stock responses which enable workers to know what to do; third, it perpetuates the category of 'dangerousness' as a blanket category which trivialises the life experiences and skills of all black people and subjects them to increased surveillance and control by white authorities (Dominelli, 1988). The dynamics of trying to manage this system and turn it in anti-racist directions only to discover that it fails to respond because 'it is too big and complicated' leads to frustration for well-meaning white probation officers and anger and frustration for black people. Meanwhile, it enables those whose inclination is to dismiss anti-racist perspectives altogether to carry on with their job regardless of poor practices. Yet it is clear that a full exploration of the role of the criminal justice system and of the Probation Service in reproducing racist dynamics is essential if workers are to become effective anti-racist probation officers and carry their organisations along the same paths.

None the less, the Probation Service as part of the criminal justice system is a site in which we are entitled to expect justice to reign. In practice, however, the experience of women, black and white, and that of black men is one of manifest injustice in the ways in which services are delivered to them and in the composition of the workforce. The specific needs of would-be black probation 'clients' are often ignored. These are exemplified by: the Nigerian women languishing in UK prisons for drug-carrying offences without due regard being paid to their specific needs (Tarzi and Hedges, 1990; Cheney, 1993; Williams, 1995); the double jeopardy experienced by black prisoners convicted of an imprisonable offence when deportation proceedings are initiated by the Home Office at the end of their sentence (CADP, 1992); the failure of main grade officers to make recommendations regarding appropriate disposals for black offenders in their court reports (Whitehouse, 1986; Denney, 1992), and the experiences of black offenders who are racially abused when placed in predominantly white community service work groups.

Women make up about 50 per cent of main grade officers, but few of them will be found at the top echelons of the labour hierarchy in probation. The picture in the criminal justice system more generally is no different (Kennedy, 1992). The situation is even more stark for black people. Black men and women are found working as main grade officers, but they are absent from the ranks of Chief Probation Officers. They are also seldom appointed as magistrates, judges or barristers (Dholakia and Sumner, 1993). Yet black men and women are disproportionately represented as inmates in custodial institutions (Hood, 1992; Sivanandan, 1992). In some situations – for example, amongst hospitalised mentally disordered offenders – black people form the overwhelming majority of inmates (Browne, 1993; Home Office, 1986; Sashidharan, 1986; Fernando, 1991). Thus black men and women are conspicuous by their scarcity as workers and conspicuous through their numbers as offenders.

How do we explain this seeming paradox at a time when there is, at least formally, so much commitment to policies advancing 'equal opportunities' and when the Criminal Justice Act 1991 (Section 95) requires the monitoring (in itself a passive act) of the criminal justice system in order to prevent discrimination?

Part of the answer lies in the passive conceptualisation of the issues to be addressed. Many of the measures introduced to ameliorate the situation focus on collecting information, monitoring behaviour and writing things down on paper. These are by and large passive acts which do not guarantee change. Indeed, since the definition of the problem to be addressed is an individualistic one, it fails to tackle the collective and structural nature of oppression and inequality. Questions of commitment and resourcing must underpin action aimed at changing personal prejudice, institutional resistance and cultural norms which foster white male supremacist social interaction. Otherwise, anti-racist initiatives will endure for only the briefest of moments.

Yet no new resources are earmarked for the purposes of changing existing arrangements and furthering egalitarianism. On the contrary, the public mood being articulated by the media and government is very much against programmes aiming to progress in these directions. We are already witnessing a powerful backlash against anti-racist initiatives in social work which is being instigated at the highest levels – the Home Office, the Secretary of State for Health, the Chair of the Central Council for Education and Training in Social Work and the Prime Minister himself (see *Observer*, 1 August 1993; *The Independent*, 4 August 1993; Cohen, 1994). This does not augur well for those interested in altering the existing political climate for the betterment of humankind.

How can grassroots action counter such a powerful group of opponents? Appealing to justice, equality and people's social conscience requires the acceptance of values supportive of anti-racist struggles. Yet the current political climate is one which gives priority to harsh, market-oriented differentials which exploit the gap between egalitarian ideals and social reality in order to discredit ideals endorsing equality between people. Changes in work routines arising from 'Punishment in the Community', the implementation of National Standards and privatisation are also contributing to the erosion of these ideals. They have done so by encouraging the assumption of resourcing priorities which pit one form of oppression against another (for example, probation officers ignoring domestic violence against black women) and attacking the professional autonomy and discretion which individual probation officers have used to push back those boundaries which seek to pathologise the victim-survivors of oppressive relationships and redefine working relationships between themselves and their 'clients'.

Hence the struggle to realise anti-racist and black perspectives in the criminal justice system is about more than the struggle to implement equal opportunities. It is about introducing a fundamental shift in workplace organisation and practices, and requires constant vigilance and action to promote and maintain its position. Sustaining the permanency of this shift requires changes in broader society too. That is why it is important to draw distinctions between policies aimed at furthering equal opportunities, anti-discriminatory practice, and anti-oppressive practice, of which anti-racism is the element focusing on 'race'-based oppression.

In our view, 'anti-oppressive practice' is an umbrella term which encompasses both equal opportunities policies and anti-discriminatory practice. It is our way of signifying that anti-oppressive practice is about holistic change, not merely change which tinkers piecemeal with various facets of the system of *oppression* which, in the case of racial oppression, black people experience *as black people*. This approach also allows for the fact that there can be more than one system of oppression impinging on a person's life at any one time – for example, as in 'race' and gender oppression shaping a black woman's life experience.

Ideally, we feel that the concept of 'anti-oppressive practice' should enable us to address simultaneously any social dimensions on which a particular individual is oppressed (see Dominelli et al., 1994). However, whilst we are able to reconceptualise this position, achieving it in practice is infinitely more complex than can be conveyed in this book. We have therefore chosen to focus on 'race', albeit covering the other social divisions such as age, disability, sexual orientation, class and gender as we encounter them in our case materials. In this sense, anti-racist practice becomes an exemplar for how other forms of oppression can be tackled in our work as practitioners and educators.

2 'Race', racism and equal opportunities: A black perspective

In 1988 the Home Office assumed a lead role in the development of race equality policies in the Probation Service. Home Office Circular No. 75/88 requires all probation committees to:

> ensure genuine equality of opportunity for people of all races involved in the work of the probation service, whether as employees, subjects of enquiry or supervision or volunteers. (Home Office, 1988, para. 1A)

It also states that:

> An effective race issues strategy must begin with a clear statement of policy by those responsible for the management of the organisation and lead to a format for regular review of progress linked to factual measurement of change. (Home Office, 1988, para. 4.1)

'Race' equality issues are, to some extent, similar in organisations of whatever kind. In Chapter 5 we focus on the practice of race relations and equality of opportunity in the Prison Service, and some of the issues there are not very different from those encountered within the Probation Service. However, there are some implications deriving from the Probation Service's role in society and the criminal justice system, its organisational structure, culture and composition of its workforce and nature of its clientele that make it special. These issues are examined from a black perspective in this chapter.

We have argued that, despite the high profiling of equal opportunities policies and the progress made by some Probation Service areas, the reality is that black practitioners still have an uphill struggle to survive in most of them. This is perhaps inevitable given what Ahmad (1990) describes as the 'power of institutionalised values and rules' and how these determine the initiation process for each entrant into this or any other organisation:

If their personal values are based on the dominant cultural values and institutional norms, then it is more likely than not that they are socialised to the mainstream institutional values and norms with greater ease than those who belong to the minority cultural groups. (Ahmad, 1990, p. 42)

On entry into the Probation Service, black practitioners are socialised into a racist culture which sometimes devalues their own humanity and leaves them feeling isolated. As one newly-qualified black probation officer expressed it:

I wonder whether this talk about relevant services to black clients is genuine. Nobody seems to realise where I am coming from. As far as they are concerned I understand black people, but I am seen as different from them. Where does this leave me?

This case illustrates the power of institutionalised values and their implications for black practitioners. This officer is expected to integrate fully into a white organisation that excludes black perspectives. But the reality is that the culture of the team and what is expected of him are at odds with his own identity and value base. In other words, this officer is being given conflicting messages, and failure to negotiate these contradictions may be interpreted as 'not being up to the job'.

How many white line managers are aware of or acknowledge these problems and how many new black workers feel secure enough to raise these difficulties with their white seniors has not yet been researched. These questions, nevertheless, raise issues which are often ignored or avoided in relationships between black staff and their white line managers. Line managers are often oblivious to the real needs of black practitioners.

In this case, the officer initially chose not to share his feelings with his white line manager for fear of being labelled a failure. However, he felt safe to do so with other black colleagues, who were able to assure him that his experience was not uncommon. He realised that institutional racism was at the root of his problems, particularly the expectation that he would be different from other black people whilst providing the necessary expertise for dealing with them. The outcome was that the officer felt empowered to initiate discussions with his line manager and team. This underlines the importance of making black practitioners' support systems an integral part of equal opportunities policies. Managers may feel threatened by black people meeting together as a group, but self-support networks are a very cost-effective method of developing their black staff and providing long-term benefits for the organisation. The raising of issues with the team brought about a better understanding of the needs of black practitioners in general. (We have focused here on white managers because the issues for black staff and black managers are different, and these will be explored later.)

The power of institutionalised values in the Probation Service has also been examined in relation to women's experience of promotion to management positions. For instance, Hayles (1989) and Kay (1993) conclude that women are under pressure to adopt institutionalised male values. However, it should be noted that most of the available literature about women in the Probation Service relates to white women, rendering black women invisible or black people genderless. There is very little recognition by both white men and women that black women are located at the intersection of racism and sexism in the Probation Service. An Assistant Chief Probation Officer, asked by a black woman about the absence of black managers in the service, replied: 'I thought you would be pleased that we have recently promoted an unprecedented number of women.' All the newly-appointed women were white. In today's politics of gender and racial equality, black women become a free-floating asset to many organisations which are capable of boasting numbers in both camps. At present, the Probation Service operates within a framework that is determined by a white, middle-class, male culture (Eley, 1989) which makes it harder for black women and men and white women to realise their full potential.

The Probation Service's capacity to transcend its integral institutional racism is further constrained by its position within the criminal justice and penal systems. It has to maintain its credibility within a very powerful, middle-class, institutionalised orthodoxy that underpins the definitions of normality and the construction of standards by which everyone is judged. This is not always obvious because debates about equality of opportunity rarely touch on cultural issues or the value base of any organisation.

The expectation that new entrants should conform to dominant values and norms can result in greater scrutiny of black practitioners' practice, as they are considered to have lower standards. Shallice and Gordon (1990, p. 47) describe how Lord Denning (1982), as Master of the Rolls, expressed a judicial view of black people in a book entitled *What Next in the Law?*, in which he claimed that 'black, coloured and brown people do not have the same standards of conduct as white'. According to Shallice and Gordon (1990), Denning's book was withdrawn and amended. At the same time, he announced his retirement amid public protests. Denning's comments may be dismissed as stemming from personal prejudice, but in our own experience, criticisms about black officers' work also centre around court reports and self-presentation in the court setting. These highlight the Probation Service's preoccupation with credibility issues at the expense of incorporating black perspectives and styles into everyday routines.

Research evidence indicates that black probation officers experience more difficulties in their probationary year than their white counterparts (Divine, 1991; Raynor et al., 1994). If it is true that black officers are given equal opportunities to demonstrate their competencies, what is it that makes them do so badly? Are they pathologically inferior, or is it cultural racism? We believe that the latter is more likely to be the case. Those who belong to marginalised cultures have an uphill struggle in resisting integration and conforming to dominant cultures (Fernando, 1991).

The conceptualisation of the notion of equality of opportunity is itself problematic. There are conceptual differences and contradictions that are rarely acknowledged and openly discussed amongst stakeholders in the criminal justice system. We will now turn to an examination of these.

Conceptualisation of equality of opportunity

Equality of opportunity is a notion that gained popularity in the UK during the 1980s. Nowadays, there is an assumption that everybody knows what is meant by it. Yet the development and implementation of equal opportunities policies are full of conceptual differences, contradictions and misunder-standings about their intended outcomes (Edwards, 1990; Fishkin, 1990; Jewson and Mason, 1993; Gibbon, 1993). The concept embraces a multitude of beliefs, expectations, attitudes and practices. Recently, the concept has become an attractive social slogan employed by different groups in the struggle for power and distribution of social and economic rewards. For instance, it has become fashionable for many organisations to call them-selves 'equal opportunities employers'. It is a 'right on' thing to have a stated equal opportunities policy. The Probation Service is no exception.

There is a diversity of views about equal opportunities policies within and across service areas regarding the employment of black people and service delivery to black 'clients'. In relation to employment, a survey carried out by the authors on equal opportunities statements in job advertisements in the *Probation Bulletin* in April and May 1994 revealed two broad categories of views. One emphasises the fairness of their selection processes and the equal treatment of all applicants, regardless of their social location in society. One Chief Probation Officer, quoted in Holdaway and Allaker (1990), vividly expressed this view as follows:

> Our policy is that appointment is not dependant on colour, creed or sex. We are not monitoring for equal opportunities because we are already doing it – acting fairly. (p. 31)

The second category gives consideration to equality between social groups as measured by proportionality of representation. It encourages applications from under-represented groups. These categories are similar to those identi-fied by Jewson and Mason (1993, pp. 218–34) in their analysis of how equal opportunities policies are conceptualised within the local authorities. They identify the liberal and radical approaches. The liberal view is concerned with the fair application of the rules of competition through bureaucratisation of procedures. In its purest form, the liberal view is only concerned with how competition is conducted. Inequalities are acceptable if they are seen to be distributed fairly. Some people believe that the fair application of rules provides a process by which an organisation can arrive at an equal distribution of outcomes.

However, most of the literature on the implementation of these types of equal opportunities policies suggests that their benefit to the excluded groups is very limited. For instance, Gibbon (1993), in a study conducted in Sheffield amongst private and public employers, found very little or no relation between the possession and implementation of equal opportunities policies and change in employment outcomes for black people. Stone (1988) comes to a similar conclusion in relation to local authorities' implementation of policies for women. Webb and Liff (1988) found that, despite an elaborate implementation of an equal opportunities policy, a United States university failed to bring about a gender balance in its workforce. This is not surprising given that the powerful groups already know and understand the rules of the game and therefore have an advantage over those the policies are intended to benefit. However, the impact of such policies is to shift the blame for inequalities away from institutional racism and sexism and onto white women and black people.

The radical conception, on the other hand, focuses on outcomes of the competition or whether there is equal distribution of social rewards among different social groups. Equality of opportunity is seen in terms of net opportunities between different groups rather than between individuals. The radical view embraces principles such as compensatory justice and proportionality. Under compensatory justice, equal opportunities policies are intended to correct past injustices done to black people. Compensatory action then becomes a method for achieving proportionality, although the reality is that, without a quota system, this is an unattainable ideal.

In the Probation Service, compensatory actions include targeting black people for certain types of training or giving black 'clients' a choice of probation officer where white 'clients' would not be given that choice. Such policies can become political minefields because, although white people acknowledge past injustices, they are not prepared to give up their privileges to improve opportunities for black people. In addition, there is a proportion of white people who experience similar inequalities to black people and feel that black people are getting a better deal than them. Sometimes this is seen as reverse discrimination by those who subscribe to the liberal view of equal opportunities policies, and it can cause a backlash from those who have previously benefited from the exclusion of black people, as exemplified by the following statement:

Equal opportunities only apply to black people in this service. Some of us who have been here for years are now at the bottom of the ladder. If you complain you are labelled a racist. (white probation officer)

This white officer objected to his management's decision to target black workers for practice teacher training, in spite of the fact that all current accredited practice teachers in this Probation Service were white. Black practitioners were further disadvantaged by their lack of practice teaching experience to qualify for accreditation under the CCETSW's requirements for the practice teaching award. Yet this kind of experience is taken into account when considering applicants for promotion.

This case also illustrates another major problem with the conceptualisation of equal opportunities policies – what Fishkin (1990, pp. 37–48) calls the 'conflicting ideals of equal opportunity'. For instance, if we accept that equal opportunities policies are primarily concerned with opportunities between groups, this conflicts with the individualised equality of opportunity which derives from the principle of merit – that is, the right person for the right job. According to this principle, the above-mentioned officer has a legitimate right to complain as the management action removed fair competition between individuals. However, the reality is that the merit system favours those who, by accidents of birth and socialisation, possess the characteristics which are valued. On the other hand, the pursuit of compensatory action in a society that believes in the neutrality and fairness of the merit system reinforces stereotypes of black people 'coming through the back door'.

These contradictions are rarely openly acknowledged. Yet, within the workplace, they can create a very hostile environment for black practitioners. For instance, a black officer who had passed a selection interview to get her job was stereotyped as having come through the back door by colleagues outside her own team. Obviously, the officer felt hurt by these comments, which meant that she could not be 'up to the job'. But her lifelong experience of racism had equipped her with strategies for dealing with such situations. She decided to ignore everything and get on with her job. Her line manager, on the other hand, saw it as his responsibility to protect her from any criticisms of her practice which undermined her self-determination. In the end, the officer felt she was being denied an equal opportunity to take responsibility for her own professional development. The underlying problem in this case can be traced back to the conception of equal opportunities policies as compensatory measures.

It is therefore not enough for those responsible for equal opportunities policies to lift them from the shelf for implementation without politicising the organisation. The service already possess structures for putting this into practice. The National Association of Probation Officers, the Association of

Chief Officers of Probation (ACOP) and the Central Probation Council have, to varying degrees, been engaged in politicising the workforce in one way or another. A corporate approach is also necessary to link inequalities in society with employment and service delivery issues. The following Practice Example illustrates why a corporate strategy is essential.

Practice Example

> A probation team highly committed to delivering an equal service to all its clients wanted a black probation officer to join their team to provide a black perspective. The service did not have any black officers, and only newly-qualified black candidates applied, along with one experienced internal white applicant. The selection procedures favoured those with experience of probation work, and the job was offered to the only white candidate, in spite of the team's expressed willingness to accommodate the needs of a new officer.

From the personnel point of view, all candidates had been given an equal opportunity to compete for the job, and the white applicant got it on merit. The team did not think that management was committed to equal opportunities in terms of service delivery to their 'clients'. The team was also concerned about lack of opportunities for black people to gain experience of probation work. Fortunately, in this case the white candidate declined the offer of the job in favour of a black candidate whom she felt was more able to offer a relevant service. In this instance, the selection procedures were fairly applied, but this did not result in the selection of the right person for service delivery to black 'clients' and communities.

Another argument that is often put forward is that appointments are made to a service area rather than a specific probation team. We would argue that such attitudes serve to perpetuate exclusionary practices.

The historical development of equal opportunities policies in the service has also influenced attitudes, expectations and the way contradictions are negotiated. The views on the progress equal opportunities policies have made to date may differ considerably between those who have been involved since the early stages of their development and those who are looking at the position for the first time. These differences may, in turn, create tensions between them. However, it is not possible to give a detailed historical account of this development here, so we provide only an overview.

Development of equal opportunities policies

The Race Relations Act 1976 provided the legal framework for the adoption of equal opportunities policies in the area of employment and service delivery to the public. The initial response of the service amounted to the establishment of good relations with the black communities and publicising the work of the service. In 1977 the Home Office only made a suggestion that probation areas with large ethnic minority populations should appoint ethnic minorities liaison officers (Home Office, 1977). Black people were seen as failing to integrate into the structures of white society.

A two-pronged intervention was necessary: to familiarise black people with probation work, and to do this effectively the Probation Service needed to learn something about them. This led to sixteenth-century-style expeditions into the dark corners of the UK, with ethnic minorities liaison officers acting as guides. Alternative methods of working with marginalised groups were still alien to the service (Green, 1987). This approach did not challenge the status quo. It was basically politically and organisationally expedient to promote cultural enlightenment. The violent protest of black people in Brixton in 1981 (Scarman, 1981) highlighted the lack of opportunities for black young people in general, but it also underlined white supremacy. Black young people's resistance to integration and conformity to white racist values was strongly condemned:

> There are already signs among some black youths, despairing of an end to white discrimination, of a disturbing trend towards a total rejection of white society and the development of a black separatist philosophy. Pride in being black is one thing, but black racialism is no more acceptable than white. (Scarman, 1981, p. 110)

It would appear that the pursuit of an alternative, non-racist lifestyle was perceived as separatist and deplored on grounds of the potential threat to white values. Although acknowledging the prevalence of racial discrimination, the pressing problem was defined as potential racial conflict. Lord Scarman also popularised and legitimised the notion of racial disadvantage, to which welfare agencies had to respond.

It was in this context that the Probation Service began to examine its role in a multi-racial society. The Central Council of Probation Committees (CCPC, 1983) recommended the development of a national policy and dissemination of good practice. Research evidence about discrimination against black people within the Probation Service began to emerge (for example, Ridley, 1980; Taylor, 1981; Whitehouse, 1978, 1980). This suggested that black offenders were more likely than white offenders to receive harsher sentences. Moreover, probation practice had contributed to this situation. Although the major task for the service was to defuse potential racial conflicts in the inner cities, there was also a recognition of the need for self-examination, without quite knowing how to proceed. White probation officers' values came under attack, and the service looked to black people to save them. Black employees began to trickle into the service as Probation

Service Officers, outreach workers and 'race' advisers. These new recruits were given enormous responsibilities, but were marginalised and not valued in the same way as those who possessed institutionalised expertise. The following quotation exemplifies the experiences of those employees:

> I was employed after the 1981 riots, and my job was basically to build bridges between the service and the black communities. I advised management on race issues, trained probation staff and magistrates, worked with black clients and monitored probation officers' SERs [Social Enquiry Reports]. You name it, I did it. I felt important then, but was I? (black Probation Service Officer)

On a different front, NAPO struggled to get to grips with 'race' equality issues and to formulate a policy on how to tackle them. NAPO's attempt to give some direction to its members finally came in 1985 (NAPO, 1985).

By this time, the few black workers who had entered the Probation Service were experiencing isolation and an uphill struggle against racism with very little support from their white managers and colleagues. In order to survive, they formed the Association of Black Probation Officers (ABPO), which was formally constituted in 1984. ABPO sought to 'promote the appropriate delivery of services to multi-racial communities and appropriate support for black staff and students' (ABPO Constitution). ABPO also began to put pressure on NAPO, whose response to racism at the time was rather disappointingly naive, in spite of commitment by individuals. It took NAPO almost five years to produce its policy on 'race' (NAPO, 1989). The Association of Chief Officers of Probation produced its anti-racist policy in 1989 (ACOP, 1989).

The Home Office played no active role at this stage. 'Race' issues were conspicuously missing from its *Statement of National Objectives and Priorities* (Home Office, 1984), in which it sought to give some direction to the work of the service. By 1985 the Home Office was under some considerable pressure to do something about the growing number of black people being processed in the criminal justice system. The Probation Service came under heavy criticism for its lack of commitment to 'race' equality compared to the Prison Service, which, at the time, gave the impression that it was doing something about 'race relations'. David Faulkner, then the Deputy Under-secretary, outlined the Home Office's view on 'race' equality issues and the Probation Service's role as follows:

> To make sure that each Probation Service is able to reach people from ethnic minorities just as effectively and to work with them just as effectively as it can with people from the white majority. Not only that it can but that it actually does. (quoted in NACRO, 1986)

It identified the following areas as needing attention: recruitment; training;

operational management of service monitoring, and evaluation of performance and management structures. Although Faulkner represented the progressive elements within the Home Office, his statement could still be interpreted as a form of 'passing the buck'. Whilst the Prison Section of the Home Office had produced circular instructions, the Probation Section had not done so. The first prison circular was released in July 1981 and was followed by an amendment in 1982 (Genders and Player, 1989). A second circular came out in 1983. The effectiveness of these policies, as we suggest in Chapter 5, has not been all that impressive, but the point is that probation guidance was not visible at that time.

NACRO (1986) criticised the Probation Service for failing to develop effective national policies on 'race'. It called on the Home Office to take a more pro-active role. Home Office Circular No. 75/88, mentioned above, was, to a certain extent, a response to these criticisms. It did create a climate for change, and some significant progress followed at policy development level, but as we all know, 'race' equality is still a long way off.

Holdaway and Allaker (1990, p. 56), in the policy review commissioned by ACOP, conclude that, within the Probation Service, there is a minority element of probation areas which is very committed to racial equality and has worked hard to implement equal opportunities policies. For the rest of the service, there is still a lot of work to be done.

The statutory duty placed on criminal justice agencies by Section 95 of the Criminal Justice Act 1991 (to avoid discrimination on grounds of race or sex or any other improper ground and requiring the Secretary of State to publish relevant information) is a welcome political acknowledgement of the existence of discrimination in the criminal justice system. However, it is not clear how the mere avoidance of discrimination can create opportunities, since there is no statutory provision to deal with inaction. It is too early to assess the impact of this provision, but we know that a similar provision directed at local authorities has failed to bring about equality in service delivery.

Section 71 of the Race Relations Act 1976 placed a duty on every local authority to make appropriate arrangements to ensure that its various functions are carried out with due regard to the need to eliminate unlawful discrimination and to promote equality of opportunity. Twelve years later, a survey of equal opportunities policies carried out by the Commission for Racial Equality (CRE, 1989) found that most of the social services departments did not have a corporate strategy. Holdaway and Allaker (1990) also identify a lack of corporate policies in the Probation Service.

Outcomes will also depend heavily on how the published information is used. The availability of information in itself does not result in equality of opportunity for the oppressed. There is a focus on outcomes, and research evidence already available reveals that black people are being discriminated against throughout the criminal justice process. Efforts and resources should be channelled towards eliminating barriers to egalitarian processes. The starting point is for the Probation Service to pay more attention to the experiences of black people within and outside the service, no matter how small their numbers. There is now a tendency in most organisations for a tokenistic representation of black people in meetings which are white-led. Participation on these terms makes it difficult for black officers to challenge the assumptions resulting from their status differences and unfamiliarity with the jargon and protocol. The danger is that such developments may give legitimacy to institutional racism and also be damaging to individual black practitioners:

> I felt that it was necessary to have a black perspective on what was taught on practice placement. But because I was not familiar with what was happening in social work education, I spent hours and hours reading all the material sent to me. Even then, I didn't think I had much to contribute. (black member of the Area of Particular Practice Planning Group)

Although this black worker did not have an equal opportunity to influence the practice curriculum, her mere presence was viewed as the inclusion of black perspectives. Some services covertly promote tokenism, as evidenced in a remark by a Deputy Chief Probation Officer in one shire county, claiming that he did not expect a black probation officer to be vocal on a Race Relations Committee. The Association of Black Probation Officers (ABPO), the National Association of Asian Probation Staff (NAAPS) and other black groups are located outside the centres of power. They are either listened to or ignored, depending on what is organisationally expedient. Formalised, systematic and regular feedback from black staff and 'clients' would act as a form of quality control on the implementation of 'race' policies.

Recruitment and retention of black staff

The purpose of recruiting black staff into the Probation Service has never been made clear. This is not surprising given the different conceptions of equal opportunities policies, what they are intended to achieve, and the conflicting expectations on black staff (Divine, 1991). The large number of black people being processed through the criminal justice system is of great concern to the white Establishment. Accusations of racism are abundant. If these black suspects and offenders were to be processed by black practitioners, this would legitimise the inequalities and shift the blame from the Establishment to the black people themselves. The proportionality principle then serves the needs of the system rather than the black people. For benefits to accrue to black 'clients' and offenders in the criminal justice system, the values that determine the processes and outcomes have to incorporate black perspectives.

Why do black people join the service? One black Home Office-sponsored student had this to say:

> Black people do not get justice in the system and I want to improve the service they get from the Probation Service.

This statement represents what some black practitioners bring to the service: a mixture of a political view and a determination to contribute towards change from within. But are these expectations realistic? The experience of first-year black officers, as described by Divine (1991), is that their black perspectives are not valued. They are judged on their ability to conform to dominant racist values. As recently as 1994, an Assistant Chief Probation Officer (ACPO) described a black probation officer in a confirmation report as follows:

> C seems to be looking for some kind of higher position eventually and he would certainly be capable of it. But he is likely to be a storm centre and may encounter and provide some unhappy episodes along the way.

Although C's future plans have not been ascertained by the ACPO, his failure to conform to institutionalised norms has sealed his fate, in spite of his competence to take on a more responsible job. For black practitioners, the ability to bring in black perspectives is an additional expectation which does not count towards competency assessment. At times, it can work against them, as this case illustrates. The ACPO's report was a blow to C, but he realised he had to develop a survival strategy. Support from other black colleagues was vital because an honest assessment of him could be made from a black perspective without prejudicing his future career development. It also empowered him to use the formal structures to challenge the report. Although self-supporting networks play an important part in empowering black staff, alternative or additional systems are necessary to equip them with skills for challenging the 'taken-for-granted' view and assumptions. Black consultants should be made available to black staff and their line managers. There should also be a system of accrediting black people's experience and expertise to avoid marginalisation.

Not all black staff want to stay and fight on. This includes volunteers, who are the most vulnerable people because they receive little support from managers. In the following Practice Example, racist white values made it impossible for a black volunteer to survive within the organisation.

Practice Example

Ali was a community worker with extensive experience of working with black communities supporting many people going through the courts, and he was often used by probation officers as a community resource. He decided he would be more effective if he trained as a probation officer. Having sought advice, he joined the local Probation Service as a volunteer to gain relevant experience to meet the entry requirements of social work training courses. Ali was the only black person on the volunteer programme. His background and experience of law enforcement in his community was different from that of white volunteers. Because he had a different approach to offending, he was labelled as lacking familiarity with accepted white-defined normality, and he was encouraged to undertake observation visits to white-dominated probation facilities. This compounded his feeling of isolation. He also became increasingly convinced that his lack of knowledge of mainstream service delivery would be an impediment to learning on the course. As a result, he abandoned the idea of becoming a probation officer altogether and left the Probation Service.

Ali's experience is not an isolated one. With the increasing numbers of black staff entering the Probation Service, retention has become one of the major concerns. This Practice Example illustrates some of the reasons why black staff leave. Isolation is a major problem, and this is compounded by a feeling of being unwanted when their own black perspectives are undervalued. It gets to a point where black practitioners feel like traitors to their own community, and wonder who they are, what they are trying to achieve, and for whom.

It is not uncommon for black staff to be challenged by black 'clients', who may expect miracles from black workers. Also, the internalisation of racism can force black people to see themselves as failures, instead of attributing their difficulties to institutional racism. Internalised racism can also create difficulties within black manager–black staff relationships (Burgess, 1993). A black manager's authority in a white organisation is subordinate to white authority. A black manager may, therefore, be viewed as either having sold out, being ineffective, or a key to open doors to equality for all black staff. A newly-appointed black member of staff was subjected to what amounted to racist scrutiny by a court-based team. His black manager suffered similar treatment from the same team. The black member of staff, instead of challenging the perpetrators of racism, expected the black manager to do it for him. Very few white managers know how to deal with internalised racism. This highlights the importance of support for black managers, who may be at the receiving end of both white racism and internalised racism. In Ali's case, the service failed to recognise that his assessment of career needs was based on white cultural values.

Finally, as we have already mentioned above, black people join the service expecting to contribute to change. This can be in sharp contrast to organisational expectations that black people will conform to racist values that define black experience as inferior (Dominelli, 1993).

Living with contradictions and unmet expectations

So far we have argued that black staff bring into the service their experiences, expectations and attitudes, as well as highlighting the contradictory positions organisations place them in. The framework within which these matters are negotiated is constructed by white values. This does not, therefore, give black staff an equal chance to develop their full potential alongside those whose values correspond with dominant cultural values and institutional norms. The concepts of equal opportunities policies do not include questions about equality of different values, and they also leave everyone confused about the role of black workers in the organisation. It is therefore tempting to ask whose purpose do equal opportunities policies on 'race' serve? How do black practitioners live with these contradictions and unmet expectations?

The reality is that, although black practitioners share common experiences and sometimes common feelings about racism, the strategies for survival are specific to each individual. These will be influenced by past experiences of racism, work environment, access to other black colleagues, management styles, availability of other support networks, and so forth. It is not acceptable to make one black worker a benchmark against which every black member of staff is judged. This can be divisive, as it sets black members of staff against each other. Moreover, white colleagues can sometimes thrive on seeing differences and conflict among black colleagues. A strategy adopted by black members of one team was to develop codes of signalling to each other if they had differences of opinion, and those differences would be sorted out outside formal meetings. This was not conspiracy but a strategy for survival. Another strategy involves being careful about what you say about other black people because it might be taken as gospel. For instance, a black member of staff confided in a white colleague that she did not like a black colleague. Although a specific reason for that was given, it was interpreted as black people disliking black colleagues.

The court setting is a very hostile environment in which black staff have to prove themselves and be accepted. The climate makes it difficult to challenge every incident of racism, and if you do, that can be detrimental to your health. Not seeing everything as one's own problem is a survival strategy that some black officers adopt. Sometimes this goes against the expectation that black people should be able to identify and confront every incident of racism. The following Practice Example demonstrates such problematic circumstances.

Practice Example

> *Dawn was three months into her first year as a probation officer. She went to*

crown court, where she sat on the probation bench. An usher came along to ask her to sit on the public gallery. She was furious and felt undermined in confidence. A few weeks after that incident she went to magistrates' court, where she was seen by the receptionist unlocking the probation office. A few minutes later, a group of court staff, including solicitors, rushed into the office suspecting that she was an intruder. Dawn's immediate reaction was that she could not cope with that kind of policing and racism. But after giving it some thought, she felt that it was not her problem and decided to ignore any racist responses to her presence. That worked well for her because she was able to concentrate on her job. Its success was confirmed by a white Administrative Officer who accompanied her to court one day and noticed that everyone in court thought she was the probation officer instead of Dawn. The Administrative Officer reported the incident to her senior. But Dawn was used to being reacted to in that way. She was not prepared to make it her problem any more, in order to survive.

This Practice Example raises the question of how far black staff can be expected to challenge racism without it taking over their personal development in other areas.

Conclusions

In this chapter we have highlighted the lack of distinct statements indicating what equal opportunities policies in the Probation Services are expected to achieve. A personnel viewpoint is that they are intended to give everyone an equal chance to compete for employment. How this is translated into equality in service delivery is not very clear. In most Probation Services, there is no link between staff selection and service delivery. Different conceptions are adopted to suit different situations. Hence, who actually benefits from equal opportunities policies is unclear. The organisation obtains some benefits from the enhanced image resulting from promulgating equal opportunities policies. The exclusion of alternative values and norms in the debates about equal opportunities policies makes it difficult for black staff to claim any benefit from the policies. They do not have an equal opportunity for professional development and to bring in black perspectives. However, some Probation Services fully support their black staff's attendance at ABPO, NAAPS and other black workers' support groups.

We believe that staff's development will be enhanced by the use of black consultants. These would be able to reach those practitioners who find group support difficult. Isolation and devaluing black perspectives and experience should be avoided if black staff are to be retained within the service. Accreditation of black experience and expertise should be introduced to improve retention of staff. Furthermore, black 'clients' and black staff should have the authority to control the quality of the implementation of equal opportunities policies.

3   Self-empowerment, empowering others and justice

Introduction

Every human being has the right to be treated with respect and dignity. All too often, however, such rights are denied to black people, and we recall that, even during training to become probation officers and social workers, the aspect of respect and dignity for others was an issue which was rarely addressed. The end result of this, confirmed by our own work and observations within the criminal justice system and by research such as that undertaken by Voakes and Fowler (1989), is that an individual's right to justice and fairness is not always upheld by those who have a duty and a responsibility to do so. What has become abundantly clear over recent years is that the colour of a person's skin (particularly if that person is black), their gender, and any noticeable disability, can often lead to that person receiving an inferior service from their probation officer or social worker to that normally received by white, male offenders.

This situation is exacerbated by the fact that those who carry out judicial functions in a court of law are exempt from any civil liability for anything done or said by them while acting in a judicial capacity (Hood, 1992). To many, this may be surprising, given that the Race Relations Act 1976 makes racial discrimination unlawful with regard to the provision of goods and services to members of the public. Indeed, many would argue that the courts are specifically empowered to serve the public, and should not, therefore, be exempt from this Act. None the less, there have been calls for the courts to be brought within the legislative framework which applies to the rest of the population. Although this has yet to occur, Section 95 of the Criminal Justice Act 1991 does at least remind those working within the criminal justice system of their 'duty to avoid discrimination against any person on the grounds of race or sex or any other improper grounds' (Hood, 1992, p. 2).

Many individuals and bodies, such as the National Association of

Probation Officers (NAPO), have argued for issues concerning 'race' to be placed on the agenda of all Probation Services for some time, yet little was achieved until comparatively recently. In fact, before 1980, the issue of racism within the Probation Service was in many respects a 'non-issue', and it was not until the inner-city disturbances of 1981 and the subsequent Scarman Report (Scarman, 1981) that attention turned to the role of the public agencies, like the Probation Service, in the UK's multi-cultural society (Holdaway and Allaker, 1990).

Anti-racist probation practice is nothing less than good probation practice, and as such it should permeate throughout the workings of the Probation Service. All too often, anti-racism is seen as being a separate entity, and has to compete for resources against other forms of oppression or other priorities which services either set for themselves or have set for them by the Home Office. Given this, and the marginalised position in which issues of 'race' are discussed, it is not too surprising to find that many probation officers are more comfortable with colluding with racism than challenging it. The answer to this problem lies in training, in particular 'anti-racism training' rather than racism awareness training or the more diffused equal opportunities training. Peter Fryer points out that:

> black people have been living in Britain for nearly 500 years. They have been born here since around 1505, and throughout their lives they have experienced racism on almost a daily basis. (Fryer, 1987, p. xi)

With this in mind, we would argue that setting up three- to four-day courses devoted solely to anti-racism training would not be asking too much of any organisation which aims to help its staff address both the past and present impact of racism.

Training

Dominelli (1988) has pointed out that anti-racism awareness training has been specifically geared towards raising white people's consciousness of racism in its many manifestations. After defining the issues, white workers are encouraged to take action in challenging racism, rather than collude with it and so maintain the status quo. For black workers, the experience of living and growing up in the UK means that their need is mainly for affirmation and assertiveness training, in order to survive in what can often be hostile environments. Black workers, however, also require anti-racism training to raise their level of consciousness so that they too can take a positive role in changing the workplace environment of the Probation Service. Anti-racism training should aim to empower workers to the point where they feel that their work 'can make a difference' to the prevailing norms of oppression. In the majority of cases, changes will be on a small scale, but they will be changes none the less. Moreover, these changes will be quantifiable, as their focus is on 'behaviour' rather than on the much more difficult task of trying to change attitudes.

Anti-racism policies and codes of practice provide a statement of commitment from the organisation about its desire to treat all people who come into contact with it on a fair and equitable basis, irrespective of the recipient's ethnic appearance, religion or culture. Although such a statement is primarily aimed at ensuring that the behaviour of staff is acceptable, its other function is to empower recipients of the service by giving them rights to redress any behaviour which they have found unacceptable. The difficulty here, however, lies in the fact that many visitors to the probation office are unaware of the existence of such policies. The policy documents themselves, though located in each office, often with each officer, are usually out of sight (and mind). Moreover, there are few accessible signs informing visitors of their rights and how to use the policy should the need arise. The 'invisibility' of many anti-discriminatory policies means that they are, in practice, ineffectual and seldom used by either members of staff or the public.

Worker–'client' relationships

A visitor's first contact with the probation office and its reception staff will determine whether or not that person feels welcomed and respected by the organisation (Holdaway and Allaker, 1990; NAPO, 1991). Posters which show positive images of black people, women and disabled people, and leaflets which have been translated into the languages of service users will give visitors an impression of the ethos of the people who are employed within that particular building. However, it must be remembered that such images are only a start and not an end to the issue of anti-oppressive practice. The apparent invisibility of a service's anti-racism policy or equal opportunities policy can be countered by teams making callers aware of the existence of such policies through the use of posters. Such action helps to empower callers by making them aware of their right to be treated with respect and dignity.

An example of a poster created by one team in the north of England, when none was readily available, contained the following message:

Racist and Sexist Behaviour

We have a policy of non-discrimination on the grounds of race or sex.

Racist or sexist behaviour and language are not acceptable and action will be taken.

If you have any queries or complaints please discuss them with a member of staff.

The aim of the poster is essentially twofold. First, it informs visitors to the office that discriminatory language and behaviour on their part will not be tolerated by the Probation Service. Second, it tells visitors that they have a right to complain should anyone else in the office, including members of staff, use language or engage in behaviour that the complainant deems unacceptable. In practice, members of the team who normally found it difficult to challenge either visitors or other members of staff about issues of racism, sexism and disablism could effectively challenge the person concerned simply by drawing their attention to the poster. The mere fact of having the poster displayed helped to raise awareness of the desired culture within the team, and in the majority of cases, the simple action of pointing to the poster would elicit an apologetic response and a change in behaviour.

Another unforeseen response was that visitors would openly own up to and remind themselves, or each other, of the unacceptability of their behaviour when it was seen to go beyond the bounds of office expectations. The team agreed that the 'action' implied within the wording of the poster could range from a verbal challenge to a refusal to work with the person whose behaviour was considered offensive. The team also concluded that, in the case of probation 'clients', 'unacceptably offensive behaviour' could lead to breach proceedings. Moreover, it meant that visitors who wilfully or persistently displayed offensive behaviour, or used offensive language excessively, would be asked to leave the office.

The area Probation Committee later adopted the poster, but significantly altered the wording so that it read as indicated in the chart opposite.

This example shows that, whilst the individual team is prepared to take 'action' with regard to challenging racist and sexist behaviour, and in practice, offensive behaviour on the grounds of disability, the area Probation Service as a whole is not. It was therefore encouraging to note that several teams chose to use the original poster rather than the probation committee-approved one. Their main reason for doing so is that the team's poster does

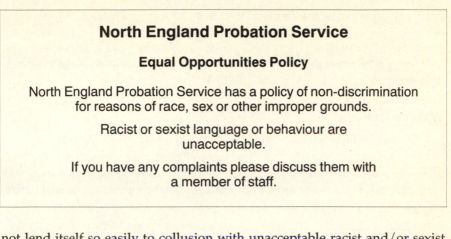

not lend itself so easily to collusion with unacceptable racist and/or sexist behaviour.

Monitoring oppressive incidents

As part of their commitment to anti-oppressive practice, some teams have a monitoring book in which incidents of a racist, sexist or other improperly discriminatory nature are recorded. A brief note of the unacceptable language or behaviour is recorded, as is the action taken by the person witnessing the incident. This record is read out during weekly team meetings so that staff can consider the incidents. This process is undertaken to offer support to the person initiating the challenge, increase the team's awareness of the type of behaviour present in the area and engender confidence amongst team members so that they will be more willing to challenge, rather than rationalise, unacceptable behaviour. The name of the person causing the offensive behaviour is not recorded, unless the incident is deemed serious enough to warrant it, because the aim of the exercise is to focus upon the process and method of challenge.

Good practice must be geared towards encouraging a change in both attitude and behaviour on both individual and institutional levels. An important stage within this process is that senior management and the probation committee are informed of all incidents, in case additional action by the service is necessary. This feeding through of information helps make higher management and the employers aware of what is happening within the team.

Report writing

So how does anti-racist probation practice work in the field? We believe everyone engaged in the criminal justice system is responsible for ensuring that their practice is both fair and anti-oppressive. Moreover, practitioners should work in the knowledge that 'our practice can make a difference'. The following is an example of how racist language was challenged by a trainee probation officer.

Practice Example

> *During an interview for a Pre-Sentence Report, the offender made a racist remark about a local shop which he had visited prior to committing the offence. The probation student, who was conducting the interview, told the offender that he felt that it was unnecessary to identify the shop by the assumed nationality or colour of the owner's skin.*

As Gill and Marshall's (1993) resource pack *Working with Racist Offenders* demonstrates, there is a danger in challenging another person's language and the attitudes which may underpin their behaviour. Thus the challenger's own safety must be at the forefront of his or her thoughts when deciding whether or not to question someone. How the challenge is received will depend upon whether the challenger is black or white, male or female, or has any noticeable form of disability. In the eyes of the person being challenged, these factors will affect the credibility of the person doing the challenging. In the Practice Example described above, the student was a white man and could have colluded with the offender's remarks instead of challenging the offender in a gentle and supportive manner.

The offender's initial response was to ask what he should have said, given that as far as he is concerned 'everyone' in the locality refers to the shop as he had done. The probation student responded that referring to the shop by its function, for example, 'the newsagent', or simply calling it 'the local shop' would suffice. Moreover, the 'client's' derogatory description of the shop had no bearing upon the nature of the offence. The offender apologised and used one of the suggested examples offered by the probation student before going on to give the details of the offence.

The example cited above is interesting for two reasons. First, it exposes the endemic nature of racism (CCETSW, 1991a) for the offender feels that his descriptive term for the shop is the norm. Second, the probation student effectively challenged the offender's language by suggesting that he provide a more 'specific' description of the shop. Alternatively, a question such as 'What did you mean when you said...?' would have encouraged the interviewee to think about what he or she had said, and how it might have been received by the interviewer. Making a request for a specific answer can be an effective method in challenging racism because it prevents the interviewee from resorting to glib stereotypes when replying.

Probation officers can make mistakes when interviewing their 'clients'. This fact needs to be recognised and shared with them. Acting in keeping with this suggestion is liberating to the interviewer, empowering to the 'client' and enabling to the worker and 'client', who can learn from each other and support one another in doing so.

Court and sentencing

Attending court is a traumatic experience for most offenders. However, the occasion may be even more traumatic if the offender is not alerted to the limitations of the Pre-Sentence Report. Specifically, the defendant should be warned that the report is an 'aid to sentencing' of which the judge or magistrate(s) may decide to take only a limited account. The reality, there-fore, is that the power to either follow or disregard the preferred sentencing option contained in the Pre-Sentence Report lies firmly with the Bench. The role of the report writer is thus to use his or her knowledge of the offender, the offence and the community in which the offender lives to influence the decision made by the judge or magistrate(s).

Given the location of power within the court setting, some workers believe that the defendant should be advised about the options available should the Bench decide to be more punitive than anticipated. This possibility arises, for example, if a custodial sentence is imposed when a community penalty might have been appropriate. If such an outcome seems likely, the report writer should inform the defendant of his or her right to appeal against the sentence. However, taking such action can become controversial, for many think that this advisory role should be left to the defendant's legal represen-tative.

The proportion of black people in prison is extremely high (see Chapter 5 for a fuller consideration of this issue). The risk of a black person ending up in prison can be up to six times higher than should be the case (Skellington and Morris, 1992). In August 1989 the Prison Reform Trust estimated that if white people were sent to prison at the same rate as black people, the total prison population would be around 300,000 rather than under 50,000 (Skellington and Morris, 1992; Hood, 1992). In light of the high risk of imprisonment that they face in comparison to their white counterparts, black defendants should be informed of the likelihood of being dealt with by way of a custodial sentence. This means discussing with black defendants how they may be seen by the court and how the colour of their skin may have a significant bearing upon the outcome of their court appearance. Given the evidence which has already been amassed in this regard, black 'clients' should be appraised of the fact that UK justice is not 'colour blind' (Smellie and Crow, 1991; Hammersmith and Fulham Borough Council, 1991; Skellington and Morris, 1992; Hood, 1992; Shallice and Gordon, 1990).

The two following Practice Examples are instances where the report writer felt that the colour of the defendants' skin would have a significant effect upon the outcome of their respective court appearances. As such, he warned both defendants that, though the court could deal with them by way of sentences which left their liberty intact, they should be aware that the colour of their skin might result in their being given custodial sentences. If such an outcome were to prove to be the case, then they should appeal against their sentence.

Practice Example

K was the black owner of two town-centre shops. Trade slumped, and K was left in serious financial difficulties after the completion of a large shopping mall on the outskirts of town. K sought help from the Department of Employment but was advised to give up the business and claim Unemployment Benefit. K followed the advice but used the money obtained in State Benefit to maintain the viability of the remaining shop, until detected by the Department of Social Security.

The report for the magistrates' court detailed K's current financial debts, lack of previous convictions, remorse, and entitlement to another form of State Benefit. A conditional discharge plus a compensation order was suggested to the court, as this would both punish and allow K to repay the money which had been falsely obtained in State Benefit. It would also enable K to continue to work and would act as a deterrent against the committal of any further offences.

The magistrates gave K two months' imprisonment and asked that it be fed back to the report writer that they thought that the suggested sentencing option was 'inappropriate'. K's appeal against the sentence was successful. The judge commented that the offence had not been 'so serious' as to warrant imprisonment. And as K had served a period in custody waiting for the appeal to be heard, the Community Service Order which he would impose would be reduced accordingly.

The second Practice Example involves A, who was black and was arrested for driving while disqualified and having no insurance. The subject of a two-year driving ban, A had recently served 18 months' imprisonment for offences of theft and was on the last few days of post-custody supervision.

Practice Example

A's sister had bought a car, which was parked while the insurance documents were being processed. A decided to drive the vehicle but was arrested by the police while doing so. The report pointed out A's remorse, few previous convictions, and the progress made during the post-custody period of supervision.

Given this, it was proposed that A be dealt with by way of a financial penalty. At the magistrates' court, A was sent to prison for three months in addition to being fined and disqualified from driving. At the crown court, the appeal was upheld, and A was instead fined and disqualified from driving for 12 months.

By way of comparison, the two following Practice Examples are cases which bear strong similarities, with regard to offending, to those of K and A. However, in both of them the defendants were white. All four cases were dealt with by the same magistrates' court (though not by the same magistrates) within a three-month period.

Practice Example

M made false representations to the Department of Social Security and obtained over £4,000 in State Benefit. At the time of claiming benefit, M was also employed as a cleaner for the local health authority. The presiding magistrate stated that there were two options open to him: either a Community Service Order or a conditional discharge. After seeking advice from the duty probation officer, who stated that M's ongoing commitments made a Community Service Order inappropriate, M was dealt with by way of a 12-month conditional discharge.

The second Practice Example relates to E, who was being supervised after release from custody.

Practice Example

E appeared before the magistrates' court charged with four offences of driving while disqualified, taking and driving a motor vehicle without the owner's consent, five offences of having no insurance, possession of an offensive weapon and failing to surrender to custody. A number of offences were committed on bail, and the last five of E's court appearances were for the theft and illicit use of motor vehicles. Response to supervision was also poor in that in the past E had offended while on probation, during community service and during the period of post-custody supervision. At the magistrates' court, E was dealt with by way of a 12-month Probation Order and was disqualified from driving for two years.

The apparent lack of consistency in sentencing prompted a probation officer to write to the Clerk of Justices, detailing the above four cases. In response, the Clerk stated that the issue of 'race' had not been a contributory factor to the sentencing outcome of the two black defendants. He then went on to state that each case was dealt with essentially with regard to its seriousness, and claimed, for example, that in A's case, the defendant had been sentenced under the old sentencing criteria, whilst E had been sentenced under the provisions of the Criminal Justice Act 1991. However, to assure the worker that the courts were taking the criticism with regard to the over-punitive sentencing of black defendants and their over-representation in custody seriously, he stated that the magistrates' court was presently undertaking a series of 'Race Awareness Training' events in order to address the issue of 'race' and sentencing.

The probation officer had offered to discuss this issue in general terms with the Probation Liaison Clerk, but was discouraged from doing so by an Assistant Chief Probation Officer, who felt it would be best if the matter went no further. The worker was also advised to discuss all future correspondence with the team manager before dispatching it to the Clerk.

The Practice Examples considered above highlight the difficulty of trying to both prove and challenge racism on an individual basis. A collective response involving the worker's team, the Black Workers' Support Group and the local NAPO branch would have provided a more effective and sustainable objection. Through this approach, the worker would have gained more support, making it more difficult for him to be 'gagged', and it would have given the issue a fuller airing. The above cases are indicative of the practice of the differential sentencing of black defendants noted by Voakes and Fowler (1989). The response itself highlights the readiness with which the Probation Service can adopt a defensive posture on issues of 'race' and the way in which power can be used to rationalise away objections and justify sentencing which many would regard as unfair. In such situations, defensiveness becomes a means by which the status quo is maintained. 'Race Awareness Training' on its own will not address unfair sentencing. A powerful group's 'awareness' of a less powerful group's 'race' or culture is no guarantee that the former will not abuse its power to control the lives and destiny of the latter group. History is replete with examples of this – the whites in their dealings with blacks in South Africa; Serbs and Muslims in Bosnia, and Nazis and Jews in wartime Europe, to mention a few.

Research suggests that if sentencers concentrated on the objective factors related to the offender – such as type and seriousness of offence(s), previous convictions, bail record, employment and age – then on average proportionally more white male offenders would receive custodial sentences than either black male or female offenders (Skellington and Morris, 1992).

The reality, however, as detailed above and elsewhere in this book, is that sentencers, the vast majority of whom are white, are more likely to deal with black offenders by means of imprisonment than they would their white counterparts (Voakes and Fowler, 1989). In the light of this, sentencers require not so much 'awareness' of different colours and cultures, but 'Anti-Racism Training'. As a consequence of this, sentencers could be asked to monitor their judgments to ensure that they do not discriminate on any improper grounds, such as 'race', sex or disability (Section 95, Criminal Justice Act 1991). A checklist might help them in carrying out this work, but it should be seen as only a first step in developing anti-racist sentencing practice. Moreover, the introduction of a checklist meeting the needs of black defendants and aiming to change sentencing practice may require legislation for it to be used in practice. The checklist could include the following questions:

- Would the sentence be different if the defendant were white?
- Would the sentence be different if the defendant were male?
- Would the sentence be different if the defendant were not suffering from a disability?
- If you were in the defendant's position, would you feel that you had been dealt with fairly in comparison with a white (able-bodied) counterpart?
- Is the sentence more punitive than is commensurate with the seriousness of the offence?

The aim of this questionnaire is to encourage a sense of 'fairness' in the sentencing process. So, if the answer to any of the above questions is 'yes', some form of re-evaluation prior to the passing of sentence is required.

Conditions attached to probation orders

Some research has shown that probation officers do not always consider the full range of schemes and sentencing options when they write reports on black offenders. Voakes and Fowler note that financial penalties are suggested more often for black offenders than for white offenders, even though structural inequalities mean that black offenders are more likely to be in receipt of either low incomes or State Benefits than their white counterparts (Voakes and Fowler, 1989).

The unwillingness of probation officers to recommend sentencing options such as Supervision Orders or Probation Orders (with or without conditions) which bring them into continued contact with black offenders suggests that some white probation officers are reluctant to work with black offenders. One reason for this reaction could be that the officer lacks the skills for working with black 'clients' (or certain black 'clients'). Another is that the officer may place too much emphasis on supposed cultural differences as opposed to 'offending' behaviour as the basis for their work. Or the officer may feel that he or she has little or nothing to offer black 'clients'. A further reason that is given is a belief that existing problems will eventually be resolved within and with the help of the offender's own community network. The end result of this 'distancing' (pushing away), is that fewer black 'clients' are likely to receive community supervision by the Probation Service than their white counterparts (Denney, 1992).

Another important new direction for the Probation Service has been that of fostering work with the voluntary sector. Here, in exchange for financial support, Probation Services have been able to tap into the knowledge and experience which voluntary organisations have developed over the years. Hostels provide long-established examples of joint work involving co-operation between the statutory and voluntary sectors. Bail assessment schemes and drug and alcohol counselling schemes represent newer examples of this trend. Working with the black voluntary sector in projects such as housing and mental health (Ohri, 1991) will challenge Probation Services to acknowledge the existence and importance of a black perspective in the joint work which they will undertake. This development will have implications for anti-oppressive practice within the Probation Service, as there will be pressure for it to adopt a less controlling but more imaginative and flexible response when working with black 'clients'. Moreover, we believe that such initiatives will improve the quality of services which are offered to all clients.

The growth in the number of probation-sponsored schemes – both in-house and through links with the voluntary sector – and the corresponding upsurge in the number of places available for 'clients' sentenced to community penalties has not altered the low numbers of black 'clients', compared to white ones, being sentenced to community penalties. This state of affairs is worrying. Moreover, the situation is exacerbated by the continued steady rise in the rate of incarceration for black people (NACRO, 1992). The Probation Services must begin to address seriously the reasons why they are failing to increase substantially the numbers of black 'clients' with whom they work in the community.

Worker–worker relationships

For many black people employed within the criminal justice system, the name of the game is still 'How do I survive in an essentially hostile environment?' The answer to this question will be particularly important if the worker happens to be the only black person employed in the team or office setting. As indicated in Chapter 5 of this book, in contrast to the 'receiving end' of the criminal justice system in which black people are over-represented as a proportion of the population, the 'delivery end' is characterised by a scarcity in the number of black people employed within the system. Organisations need black members of staff to help them develop new services which are relevant to the needs of previously-excluded groups, including black ones, and to improve existing services to meet the needs of the community as a whole (Rooney, 1982). Unfortunately, the current situation is that black people pay their taxes on an equitable basis with white people, but often get an inferior or oppressive service in return.

The number of black people employed within the criminal justice system has gone up since 1988. But the picture is still essentially one of under-representation and isolation. Given this, the role of black worker support groups (a subject covered in greater detail in Chapter 2) acquires a valued importance for those attending meetings. They are particularly useful to members who are being oppressed to the point where their working lives are intolerable. Black worker support groups have fought for recognition within their employing service on the grounds that the service cannot provide the type of support which many black members of staff, at all grades, feel they require. Some Probation Services have responded to this need and allow such groups to meet during working hours. In practice, there may be times when individuals feel that pressure is being placed on them not to attend meetings. To counter this, some services have asserted that the time, and where necessary the facilities, should be made available for black workers to attend group meetings, both locally and regionally, and that this should be seen as a right and not as an extra (APS, 1992; WYPS, 1994).

Safe working environments

The conditions of employment for both black and white members of staff within any organisation can be ameliorated by the creation of a safe working environment. In principle, this means the creation of a climate in which workers are prepared to listen to and treat each other with respect and dignity. The establishment of such conditions is undermined by workers and 'clients' who commonly use racially offensive language, even if white colleagues rely on more sophisticated techniques in doing so (NAPOWYPSB, 1987). Some white workers find the prospect of challenging their white colleagues who make racially offensive remarks daunting. More than one worker has been accused of being 'over-sensitive' or of 'doing more harm than good' for taking up the challenge. The implication of such responses is that the problem would go away if people would stop talking about it. In one extreme case, a white worker who was trying to ensure fairness in treatment for black 'clients', was called a 'traitor' to her 'race' by one of her white colleagues (NAPOWYPSB, 1987, p. 10).

In 1986, NAPO established its National Anti-Racism Monitoring Committee as a result of the growing concern over the use of discriminatory language by some speakers in their addresses at meetings. By monitoring the content of meetings, the Monitoring Committee's aim was to reduce the occurrence of unacceptable language at NAPO meetings. However, monitoring has not been without its problems, as some deem the practice 'political correctness' – a matter of not saying the wrong thing at the wrong time. Thus some workers consider such monitoring a block to the free flow of discourse and a hindrance to the process of learning from each other. Those who have been on the receiving end of the monitoring process have found it an 'isolating' experience. And, in more than one instance, monitoring has acted to deter past and potential speakers from contributing to meetings. To others, however, monitoring is seen as a tool for encouraging participants to avoid the use of offensive language and behaviour, and it recognises the fact that, over the years, good intentions have not been enough to avoid collusion with and reinforcement of oppressive practice. For example, one speaker who used the word 'denigrate' at a NAPO conference before it was publicly pointed out that the word has its roots in slavery viewed it as a learning experience, which demonstrated how ignorance can contribute to the devaluing of black people's contributions to society (personal communication to authors).

Support groups

Individuals, black or white, who assertively challenge racism can find it an onerous and isolating task if no one else in their team or area shares their values or concerns about the injustice that they see around them. Such individuals can benefit from banding together to form support groups. The aims of such groups are to ensure that the issue of anti-racism is placed on team or area agendas and that the subject is addressed. In addition, individual members are helped to cope better with the stress of working in unsupportive environments if they are able to share with each other knowledge, ideas and strategies for improving the service and facilities offered to black 'clients' and colleagues. The idea of black and white people working together for the common good of eradicating oppression is not a new one. Fryer (1984) notes that the former slave, Olaudah Equiano, a writer, speaker and major force in the Slave Abolitionist Movement, was a friend and associate of Granville Sharp, the emancipationist who chaired the Quaker Society for the Abolition of the Slave Trade. Another close friend and associate of Equiano was Thomas Hardy. Hardy clearly saw the link between oppressed white people and oppressed black people, for he was the first to state that 'black freedom and white were two sides of the same coin', a message which many still believe holds true in the UK of the 1990s (Fryer, 1984, p. 106).

Black support groups

Many black probation officers feel that their greatest problems do not arise through their interactions with white 'clients' (over whom they generally have power) but in their dealings with their white colleagues and managers, people with whom they have equal or less power. The Association of Black

Probation Officers (ABPO) was set up by black workers to act as a work-based organisation which would enable its members to both resist and challenge racism. The primary function of ABPO and the National Association of Asian Probation Staff (NAAPS) is to provide work-based support for their members. As a result of the low number of ethnic minority staff and trainee staff within the Probation Service, support for individual members may have to be sought on a regional or even a national basis. A secondary function of these organisations is to raise awareness about issues of unfair discrimination and cultural bias within the Probation Service, and to draw attention to the impact that these issues bring to bear on both workers and 'clients' within the criminal justice system. Thus, in their differing ways, both ABPO and NAAPS seek to address the issue of racism within the Probation Service. (NACRO, 1991).

The usage of the term 'black' in its political sense is itself a highly controversial matter amongst 'black' people. Some black organisations – for example, ABPO – have used the term in its political sense to encompass all 'black' people who are racially oppressed by white people, regardless of their skin colour. ABPO therefore aims to challenge racism and oppose oppression within the workplace for both staff and 'clients'. Other 'black' organisations – for example, NAAPS – are concerned that the grouping together of such a vast variety of different peoples with dissimilar languages, traditions, cultures and religions will result in the specificity of their experience being lost. Hence they have opted for their own representation, which they feel enables them to engage with cultural oppression more effectively.

Whilst we accept that some individuals use the term 'black people' in a way that denies their differences, we feel it is important to both recognise the heterogeneity of 'black' people and acknowledge the importance of racial oppression as a common thread in their life experiences. Hence, using the term 'black people' in its political connotation to signal a commonly shared experience – being at the receiving end of racism – seems appropriate to us. Moreover, we are concerned that in a society permeated by racism, the internalisation of white supremacist values, including those of valuing lighter-coloured skin, can cause divisions amongst 'black people' which can be readily exploited by white supremacist organisations. The lack of agreement over terminology can further confuse a complex situation. We would therefore argue for clearly spelt-out definitions of the terms that are used.

Some members of the Probation Service consider it advantageous to separate out the different minority ethnic groups which have contact with the criminal justice system, in order to target limited resources more accurately at the 'appropriate' group(s). Arguments which support this stance come from research which suggests that, for example, West Indians, Guyanese and Africans are treated differently by the criminal justice system compared to offenders whose ethnic origins are Indian, Pakistani or Bangladeshi. A major problem in this position is that the categories used by the different organisations which operate within the criminal justice system have no agreed definitions. Some of these have listed as many as 58 different categories in an attempt to cover the ethnic origins of 'clients' that have contact with the criminal justice system (WYPS, 1994).

In opposition to the above categorisation, some workers argue that such a policy merely serves to mask a strategy of 'divide and rule' over black people. In it, one sub-group may label one or more other sub-groups as 'the problem' and compete with them for already scarce resources. Furthermore, such categorisations imply that 'white' people are portrayed as a homogeneous entity, whilst the 'black' sub-groups are presented as both numerous and 'the problem'. However, even this impression is breaking down. Sections of the UK police have gone one step further and questioned the homogeneity of white people. They have divided Europeans into two categories – 'White European' and 'Dark European' (West Yorkshire Police, 1991). This seems like another ploy which creates an artificial barrier between the group which sees itself as being 'really white' and holding power, whilst others in their midst are now defined as being different on the basis of their darker skin, and thereby seen as inferior.

The issue of 'race', ethnic monitoring and categorisation within the UK context remains a contentious one, both for those who are being categorised and for those doing the categorising. Many people are still alive who bore witness to the Second World War. They are aware of the use to which the Nazi Party put the ethnic information which it had collected about the Jewish population. Moreover, others fear that history is repeating itself – for example, with regard to the 'ethnic cleansing programmes' in Bosnia. Irish people have also been defined as 'outsiders' who can be racially exploited. Genocide and legally sanctioned murder have meant that those at the receiving end of such ministrations view with a great deal of suspicion the need to collect racially sensitive information. It may be used to liquidate them or otherwise jeopardise their survival. Such information may also be used by the State to exercise other less dramatic forms of social control. Given that the Home Office has been the major force behind ethnic monitoring in this country, and actively involved in deporting black members of the community from the UK since the late 1960s, their circumspection is justified and lends credence to demands that worries about who controls the information gained through ethnic monitoring be taken seriously.

Working with other professionals

Problems can arise when working with individuals from other professions, particularly as, more often than not, those individuals will have a different value base to that held by probation officers. As a result, when conflicts arise over the unacceptability of racially offensive language or behaviour, proba- tion staff often find that they have to resolve the matter themselves or rely upon their managers to remedy the situation. However, in the latter instance, additional tensions can be created if the manager's definition of 'appropriate action' (or inaction) falls well short of what is expected by the worker. Such interventions will leave the worker – particularly if the worker is the victim of the abuse – feeling dissatisfied and disillusioned with the lack of commitment displayed when the organisation is called upon to address issues of racism.

To remedy situations like those cited above, Probation Services have to develop strategies and procedures for dealing with and challenging racist language and behaviour. Such strategies and codes of practice are currently being developed by some teams. The better ones amongst these include a step-by-step guide to how the worker should deal with racist incidents arising from their contact with 'clients', other workers within the organisa- tion and workers from other organisations. These strategies and codes of practice have to be worked out with care if they are to fit into the service's existing disciplinary and grievance procedures. The ultimate sanctions implied in these are that wilful and persistent racially offensive language and/or behaviour could lead to breach proceedings in the case of 'clients', or dismissal in the case of staff.

Challenging workers from other organisations may be somewhat prob- lematic, but ideally, managerial representation should be made to the other person's organisation for the matter to be resolved. Initiatives such as these are ameliorative – that is, they do not transform existing power relations, but they can shift the balance of power slightly more in favour of oppressed people. Ultimately, however, anti-racist and black perspectives demand the elimination of racism from society. Achieving this aim requires fundamental social change.

Working in co-operation with professionals from within the personal social services is, more often than not, a positive experience. Attending court or going to case conferences are occasions at which probation officers get the opportunity to work closely with others. Many probation officers and social workers find attending court a daunting experience. However, we feel that workers should take comfort in the knowledge that they probably know more about the 'client' than other professionals in the courtroom. This is more likely to be so if the client has previously been the subject of some form of statutory supervision. As one lawyer notes: 'I have seen magistrates' minds completely changed when the probation officer is put in a witness box and counsel asks for his/her views on the defendant' (Hammersmith and Fulham Borough Council, 1991, p. 23).

Mental health issues

Within the mental health field, concern has been expressed at the high level of custodial remands and the compulsory detention of black offenders under mental health legislation. The National Association for Mental Health (MIND) has found that Afro-Caribbeans are over-represented in referrals made under Section 136 of the Mental Health Act 1983 (that is, referrals made by the police in connection with mentally disordered persons found in public places), not only in terms of their numbers in the general population, but also in relation to other forms of psychiatric referrals and admissions. In his research, Fernando (1991, 1993) found that 'Afro-Caribbeans are more likely to be admitted under compulsory sections than their white counter-parts'. Copes's (1989) study showed that young people of Afro-Caribbean origins born in the UK were four times more likely to be committed for detention under Part III (criminal proceedings) of the Mental Health Act than their white counterparts. Moreover, this figure rose significantly for Afro-Caribbeans who had migrated to the UK. They were up to 25 times more likely than their white counterparts to be detained under the Mental Health Act (Browne, 1990, pp. 5–6 and 40–1).

The following Practice Example looks at some issues relating to mental health.

Practice Example

D is a 23-year-old Afro-Caribbean male with a history of mental illness. He was charged with the offence of grievous bodily harm (on his 18-month-old son) and two minor motoring offences. D told the probation officer that he had not committed the offence against his son, but he had pleaded guilty to the charge on his solicitor's advice. The Pre-Sentence Report argued for a Probation Order to address D's parenting skills, offending behaviour and to ensure that he received appropriate medication. However, at his court hearing he was given 3 months' imprisonment, disqualified from driving and fined. He was later released on bail pending his appeal hearing at the crown court.

At D's appeal hearing, two further charges of assault (again involving his son) were brought against him by the Crown Prosecution Service. Initially, he was remanded in custody, but was later transferred to the secure ward of a local psychiatric hospital. D stated that he had not committed the new offences, as his bail conditions had prevented him from seeing his son. However, he again pleaded guilty to the offences on his solicitor's advice (to get them over and done with).

At court, the judge was thinking in terms of a custodial sentence, for he asked the psychiatrist about the provisions for D's treatment, either under the terms of a Hospital Order or at the end of a custodial sentence. The psychiatrist stated that D's mental illness was not severe enough for him to be Sectioned, and that, following release from custody, there would be no obligation on D's part to take medication.

In the witness box, the probation officer informed the judge that no report detailing the new offences had been submitted to the court because of D's denial of having committed the offences, and that his plea of guilt had been submitted on his solicitor's advice. The worker also informed the judge that he had not recognised much of the picture of D painted by the Prosecution, as it did not correlate with his own view and knowledge of D as detailed in the Pre-Sentence Report. The judge acknowledged what was said and then looked to the Prosecution for evidence in relation to the new offences, but none was forthcoming.

The psychiatrist was asked to return to the witness box, and the judge sought assurance on the type of programme and medication D would be subjected to during a period of psychiatric treatment. After the required information had been provided, D was made subject to a two-year Probation Order with a Condition of Psychiatric Treatment for the full length of the order.

The above Practice Example helps to illustrate some of the positive work which can be undertaken between different agencies working together within the criminal justice system. In the above case, the probation officer and the psychiatrist used their judgement to organise a treatment programme which would address D's offending behaviour and which would ensure and maintain his stability within the community. The Practice Example also highlights the fact that those who have the most knowledge of the 'client' can use that information to effectively challenge others, and by so doing aid both justice and fairness. Not to have challenged the information supplied by the Prosecution (or the lack of it) would clearly have aided the expedience of the court. However, both the probation officer and the psychiatrist believed that justice was of far greater importance than expediency, and both had no doubts whatsoever that expedience would have led to D being imprisoned.

Worker–employer relationships

Until comparatively recently, many Probation Services were reluctant to accept the existence of racism within UK society. Even when they did accept it, they were far more willing to grasp and promote the diffuse notion of 'equal opportunities' (an issue discussed more fully in Chapter 2) than anti-racism itself. Consequently, more than one turgid anti-racism policy which members of staff, both black and white, have found to be of little use has been produced. Added to this has been the unwillingness of staff to put such policies into effect. Moreover, in some instances the organisation has colluded with those deliberately flouting or ignoring these policies. A major weakness of Probation Services' equal opportunity and anti-racism policies is that they usually address the interaction between the organisation and service users, without considering the internal problems and difficulties which may arise when relationships between different members of staff break down. To resolve such matters, staff usually have to resort to the adversarial process enshrined within existing complaints and grievance procedures.

Most Probation Services, and many other organisations in the UK, state that they are 'equal opportunity employers'. However, a cursory glance at the ethnic minority composition and gender of their staff, and the levels at which the majority of those staff are employed, shows that most employers are still merely 'attempting to become equal opportunity employers'. Yet organisations use the notion of 'equal opportunity' to project an image of themselves as 'fair'. On face value, they convey a desire to treat all employees on an equitable basis. However, their statement of 'equal opportunity' may represent nothing more than fine words on paper, or at best a dilution of purpose. If the organisation is seen by either its employees or outsiders to have failed to recognise and take account of the unequal starts and positions people have in life, and that these are all affected by issues of 'race', gender, disability and class, these words are hollow.

An area of concern for many workers is the 'individualisation of oppression' (an area discussed more fully in Chapters 2 and 5). Organisations do this by distancing themselves from oppressive behaviour by claiming that the responsibility for such acts lies not with the organisation, but with certain individuals who work on behalf of the organisation. For this reason, many agencies have chosen to focus their training on anti-discriminatory practice, rather than on anti-oppressive practice. The aim of this training is to ensure that employees do not discriminate unfairly and so infringe the relevant provisions in the Disabled Persons Act, the Sex Discrimination Act and the Race Relations Act, as this could have serious legal implications for the employer. However, if an agency colludes with or fails to challenge individuals who discriminate unfairly, then the aggrieved person may feel that the organisation as a whole is oppressive and discriminates unfairly.

A major failing of the above strategy is that it takes no account of the 'ideology of superiority' – that is, 'cultural racism' (Davies and Ohri, 1994; Dominelli, 1988). As such, the value base of the organisation – which has been both consciously and unconsciously taught, and which continues to be reinforced by language, the media, professional values, the political and legal systems, and the notion that 'might is right' – is largely left untouched. As a result, the organisation continues to see black people as inferior to white people, women as inferior to men, and disabled people as inferior to able-bodied people. Given this, and the prevailing consensus which often allows negative attitudes and stereotyping to go unchecked and unfair discriminatory behaviour to be challenged only in a tiny minority of cases when it is seen to infringe legislation, it should come as no surprise that equal opportunities policies have brought little change to the status quo in many organisations.

The unwillingness of many workers within the criminal justice system to challenge its dominant value base has led to a situation whereby the whole of it can be regarded as being manifestly unfair towards black people and those who lack power. The fact that black people are over-represented as both remand and sentenced prisoners often causes the police, magistrates and judges to become defensive on an individual basis and claim that they are not responsible for the current situation. The response to this stance has to be: 'Who *is* responsible?' The answer is that the judicial system as a whole is responsible for the current results of their interventions. However, there has to be an acknowledgement that some groups who work within the system have more power than others, and that those groups also have more opportunity to use and abuse their power against less powerful sections of the community. Some workers believe that the Probation Service has a vital role to play within the criminal justice system, but believe that the organisation's unwillingness to challenge its own value base leaves it with the power, but not the will, to improve its treatment of black people.

Supervision

For black or white staff new to the service, the initial probationary period can be both vulnerable and traumatic. To 'toe the line' within often highly subjective parameters appears to be the order of the day (Raynor et al., 1994). The standard of supervision provided by white managers with regard to black workers can vary markedly, and will depend upon whether or not the manager feels comfortable in looking at the issue of 'race' and the impact that racism has had upon both the worker and the organisation. If the issue of 'race' is not addressed or acknowledged by white managers, black workers may feel that a central part of their persona is being ignored or avoided. Black workers faced with such a situation must ask themselves how much help or support they can expect to receive from their white managers. If the answer to that question is 'none' or 'very little', then the worker will undoubtedly have to continue to gain his or her main source of support from either work-based support groups or through networks outside the organisation.

Few white managers will have been on the receiving end of either racist abuse or behaviour. However, anti-racism training geared towards supervising black members of staff should give white managers the confidence they need to discuss issues regarding 'race'. Black managers, on the other hand, arrive with both the experience and a number of survival strategies for operating in racist environments. It is therefore easier for such managers to empathise with black members of staff who may be experiencing problems similar to those which they have already been through.

Relative oppression

People who feel that they are being oppressed may come to the conclusion that they are living on a different planet to those who have privilege and power. Unfortunately, some attempts to bridge the divide by those who wield power can take on the appearance of being nothing more than a game. The following Practice Example is a case in point.

Practice Example

A senior manager arranged to meet the black members of staff in order to discuss their concerns about working within the organisation. During the meeting, members of staff gave examples of racist behaviour to which they had been subjected. The manager helpfully suggested that such incidents should be reported to the probation committee, but then went on to say that staff should 'choose' to send to the committee only those incidents which would make the most impact. The black members of staff pointed out that every racist incident made an impact on the sufferer, and that staff should not have to rank their oppression or argue with each other over who had suffered the most.

Lack of understanding about how people feel as a result of their circumstances is reflected in other forms of oppression. This situation is illustrated in the next Practice Example.

Practice Example

A senior manager asked a white probation officer with a disability about the possibility of being registered as a disabled person. It soon became clear, however, that registration would be in the Probation Service's interest, as the number of disabled staff employed by the organisation was well below the 3 per cent quota of the total workforce required under the Disabled Persons Act. The manager was told that, as appointment had been on merit and in fair competition with other applicants, the worker now had no desire for a change of status within the organisation.

Members of staff who feel that they have been unfairly treated by their colleagues may have to pursue their desire for justice through grievance procedures. Sadly, grievance procedures become an adversarial contest, at the end of which there are winners and losers – an outcome which may leave issues of justice and fairness unresolved. Any individual who attempts to challenge the behaviour of the organisation which they have found to be unfair will be up against a huge power bloc. High status within an organisation does not necessarily mean that the individuals holding it have a good grasp of the issues relating to anti-oppressive practice. A way of ensuring a fair hearing is to call on two or more independent adjudicators who have some knowledge of the issues to be discussed. However, in our experience, some organisations have turned down such requests on the grounds of either cost or a lack of time. Such responses leave the aggrieved person feeling at a disadvantage even before the grievance hearing has begun.

The coupling of high status within an organisation and a poor understanding of anti-oppressive practice is an important issue. For example, at a grievance hearing, several witnesses gave details of the racist behaviour of one of their white colleagues. A black probation officer present was concerned to hear a member of the probation committee dismiss the incident as 'the odd comment' which 'would not upset'. Clearly, racist comments seldom worry the perpetrator, but they do upset the victim. The following Practice Example helps to highlight the difficulty that black members of staff can face when they attempt to challenge what they see as unfair behaviour.

Practice Example

> *Robert, a black worker, informed the grievance panel about the oppressive behaviour he had been subjected to whilst working in a team of white probation officers. He cited his experience as being from a black perspective (that is, how he viewed the situation as a black person) and placed that experience within the context of black people and their involvement with the criminal justice system. A senior manager, however, told Robert that he believes that a black perspective is really a 'selfish perspective'.*

Robert was left wondering if the white manager was engaging in an act of transference, and concerned about the implications of such attitudes for other black members of staff.

Promotion

The majority of black members of staff within the Probation Services are employed at the lower end of the hierarchy. In October 1994, no black person was employed above the level of Assistant Chief Probation Officer (Burgess, 1994). Promotion within any organisation is invariably seen as being a sign of progress, as it provides the individual with more opportunity to influence others and brings with it greater responsibility and financial reward. However, black members of staff often find that their progress is barred by subjective obstacles which limit their life chances. Examples of such barriers can range from being told that 'You have just missed out. You will have to try a little harder next time' to wholesale shifts in the goalposts, where applicants are made to feel that they do not have the right attributes for the positions for which they have applied. Similar limitations have been experienced by women and disabled people (Eley, 1989; Morris, 1991; Oliver, 1990). The overall effect of this form of exclusion, despite the introduction of job specification and person specification criteria, is that black people are still under-represented in the managerial structures of the Probation Service.

For the Probation Service to focus purely on its intention to encourage more black members of staff to become managers is not good enough, particularly if the result is nothing more than the continuation of the status quo. Makeda James (1992) argues that, in any consideration of racism, it is the outcome – a measurable factor – rather than the intention which counts. Outcomes are more difficult to achieve, but they represent the true litmus test of good intentions.

To progress within the organisation, black people have to be deemed acceptable to the body politic of their employers and prospective colleague managers. Progress to the stage of acceptability is, in essence, a gatekeeping process, whereby potential managers have to prove that they can 'fit in', hold the line, and maintain existing standards in the interest of the organisation (Rattansi, 1992). By and large, these are desirable attributes, but if to 'fit in' also means that the new manager has to become increasingly oppressive in a bid to maintain control, then seniority will bring with it a distancing from former colleagues, a degree of isolation, a lack of immediate support, feelings of insecurity and defensiveness. However, a good manager, irrespective of 'race', gender or disability, should be able to avoid some of these pitfalls by remembering to treat others with respect and dignity.

Survival

To survive with dignity in any organisation, black people must be prepared to challenge injustice where they find it. In pursuing this goal, research and information are vital ingredients in presenting their case. Moreover, addressing the issue systematically will help to broaden it out and increase its relevance to other members of staff who may be in a similar position. However, as stated earlier, the act of challenging can be a weary task, so an element of choice has to be exercised when deciding if and how the challenge should be made. A 'shared challenge' or claim for justice supported by an individual's colleagues and trade union has a greater chance of success than one that an individual pursues alone. However, some black workers now have such little faith in Probation Service-administered justice that they believe the only way to obtain fairness is to seek it by way of bodies outside the Probation Service. This situation should clearly be of concern to us all.

Conclusions

The principle of treating others with fairness and dignity is one that we would wish to be applied to ourselves if we were in our 'client's' shoes. It is a simple one to state, and is based upon having respect for ourselves and each other. However, for many workers within the criminal justice system, it is a principle with few subscribers and one which, in practice, is difficult to achieve. By empowering oneself and others, we believe it is possible to go beyond mere talk of good intentions, to address bad practice and, hopefully, attain fairness and justice. We believe that workers can make a difference in such situations if they are prepared to use their skills and knowledge to challenge the status quo and ensure that good practice prevails. Tackling issues of racism and other forms of oppression – be they in relation to 'clients', colleagues or the organisation itself – can be a difficult and weary task. For this reason, creating support groups and safe working environments, for both black and white workers, is of such importance.

If the Probation Service as an organisation is concerned about the unfair and discriminatory nature of the criminal justice system, then it must grasp the issue of anti-racism (and anti-oppressive practice) rather than merely the notion of anti-discriminatory practice. This will involve the service taking a closer look at its own performance and behaviour in relation to not only black 'clients' but also black members of staff on such issues as fairness of opportunity, supervision and promotion. This work has to be undertaken to increase the level of confidence which black people have in the Probation Service.

Black workers have much to offer as a result of the different perspectives and insights which they bring to their work. The Probation Services should view this in a positive light, as it can only help to improve the quality of service given to black 'clients' and the community as a whole.

4 Training: Opportunities and dilemmas

Introduction

Training has been a contested field in social work education since its inception as a profession (Sibeon, 1991; Dominelli, 1994). Key aspects of the controversy have focused on whether professional training should concentrate solely on the acquisition of the technical skills for 'doing the job' or whether it should allow for a broader model encompassed by liberal education. Sadly, both these approaches have neglected anti-oppressive practice in general and anti-racist practice in particular.

In this chapter we examine the absence of anti-racist perspectives in social work training and argue the necessity of their inclusion at all levels of training – pre-qualifying; qualifying and post-qualifying – regardless of whether these are delivered 'in-house' or at college. We define training *not* as the mechanistic reproduction of learnt knowledge, but as a systematic form of consciousness-raising which includes both the critical examination of existing knowledge and skills and a developmental dimension which encourages students to identify gaps in their knowledge and skills base by drawing on 'clients'' experiences of services and their own aspirations for the constant improvement of social work theory and practice.

Conceptualised in this manner, training engages with worker–'client' relationships; relationships between workers themselves, and employer–employee relationships. In the first of these, the worker's aim is to obtain and *listen to* 'client' feedback on the services which are being provided. Such an approach enables the worker to gain a sense of the forms of oppression that are being reproduced in the worker–'client' relationship. In the second, workers can facilitate learning amongst themselves and assess shared training needs which can be passed on to management in order to make the required arrangements. It is also the point at which good practice can be exchanged. Finally, training must be seen as workers' engagement in a constant process of training and retraining throughout their careers. Training, therefore, should be considered as part of employees' working conditions which the employer has a responsibility to fulfil as part of good employment practice.

Establishing relevance: Anti-racist social work practice with white people

Anti-racist practice developed out of a necessity to change service delivery to black people because provisions were inappropriate. It aims to offer a model of anti-oppressive practice applicable to all who want or are obliged to have contact with social or probation services. In other words, anti-racist practice was to be central to all 'good practice':

> Anti-racist practice is not simply about adding on 'race' components or about working with black people. It is applicable to caring sensitive work with black and white, men and women. The emphasis of 'good practice' is on making the delivery of anti-racist services to the whole community a reality. It is not about treating everyone the same, but about taking account of different needs and different realities. (Ohri, 1988, p. 1)

This key aspect of anti-racist practice has been lost; anti-racist practice has become synonymous with work with black people, and is reflected in the training received by practitioners.

This carries the danger that white people may think that, as long as anti-racist work deals with improving service delivery to black people, they have dealt with the issue. Yet the majority of white workers will work primarily with white 'clients'. Anti-racist training and practice must address this reality and seek to counter the view that white people can abdicate their responsibility to work on themselves and each other. In this chapter we will consider what white students and practitioners need to do to support and develop good anti-racist practice amongst themselves. Focusing on the needs of white students and practitioners facilitates the recognition of the fact that, in a UK context, racism is a white phenomenon. Therefore, responsibility for working out anti-racist responses lies with white people.

We feel strengthened in this view by virtue of knowing that black communities are scattered in small pockets throughout England, Wales, Scotland and Northern Ireland. The majority of social service and probation workers will have infrequent direct contact with black people as service users. On this basis, many of them will subscribe to the view that 'race' is not a problem in their area, and anti-racist practice is not relevant to their work. The 'broad-brush' anti-racist training provided by agencies concentrates exclusively on work with black people, thereby fostering the illusion that the majority of white workers will not have to address racism. In these circumstances, training that will establish the relevance of anti-racist practice throughout the country, regardless of whether or not black people live in any particular locality, is urgently required. This means stressing the importance of white workers working with white users to address racism in predominantly white communities.

Greater concentration on anti-racist practice with white people should complement, not replace, training aimed at delivering services to black people. The intention is to bring an anti-racist practice agenda into *all* work undertaken by professionals.

The extent to which training has an impact on practice remains a matter of controversy. Thompson (1994) suggests we have now reached the stage where greater consciousness of oppression and discrimination has been achieved. He cites the range of literature and training courses available, the development of embryonic equal opportunities policies and the regulations relating to social work qualifying courses as evidence for this claim. Yet the establishment of anti-racist training and practice remains vulnerable.

Consensus about the style, content and purpose of anti-racist training is lacking (Luthra and Oakley, 1991; Holdaway and Allaker, 1990). Others maintain that anti-racist social work training risks going 'over the top' (Francis, 1994) or has become too concerned with 'consciousness raising and indoctrination' (Coleman, 1988, p. 16). There are three key issues in anti-racist training which we feel trainers must address:

- the introduction of anti-racist social work practice as a requirement of the Diploma in Social Work;
- the haphazard way in which anti-racist training matches (or does not) practice realities;
- the assumption that anti-racism is a matter which concerns only working with black people.

The common theme of the three issues is the dissonance many practitioners experience when they contrast the repeated statements regarding the importance of anti-racist practice with its limited impact on their daily working lives.

With the introduction of the Diploma in Social Work (DipSW), the Central Council for Education and Training in Social Work (CCETSW), took a more assertive stance on anti-racist course content. We will examine reactions to the changes CCETSW made, and review the evidence which justifies this change. The reactions of those opposing the introduction of the anti-racist requirement confirm the view that too much attention makes anti-racist practice a fad – a form of 'political correctness'. Labelling anti-racist practice 'politically correct' has become abusive because it is itself dogmatic and oppressive, and undermines anti-racist practitioners.

Practice Example

> *A black client lodged a complaint against a white worker. This became the subject of much debate amongst white probation workers. Some said anti-racism had 'gone too far'. White workers were at risk of unsubstantiated allegations of racism and would be disciplined by managers unfairly. When asked by other workers to offer evidence supporting their view, none was forthcoming. No one could name a white worker from their own or any other district they had worked in who had ever been disciplined following an allegation of racism.*

This Practice Example indicates how white practitioners exaggerate claims of progress in dealing with racism, and magnify their fears. Moreover, such reaction reflects how, on leaving social work courses, many practitioners have found the emphasis given to anti-racism during training absent from the 'reality' of practice. Support and encouragement may depend heavily on luck, how much a senior knows or cares about the issue, and the commitment of colleagues. New white workers working in anti-racist ways may find that they are tolerated by colleagues, with the expectation that they will run out of steam and become better assimilated into the prevailing custom and practice. This reaction should be addressed during in-service training, supervision and daily practice.

CCETSW's anti-racist initiatives in qualifying training: The Diploma in Social Work

The publication of reports revealing the widespread extent of the impact of racism in the Probation Service (see Taylor, 1981; Divine, 1991) and social services more generally (see ADSS, 1978; Dominelli, 1988) combined with relentless pressure from black people and white anti-racists (see Patel, 1994) prompted CCETSW to introduce an anti-racism policy which made anti-racist training a requirement for social workers qualifying under the Diploma in Social Work (CCETSW, 1991, p. 6).

The Diploma in Social Work's first student cohort began their studies in 1990. However, the initiative was soon to become a political football as a result of opposition to the anti-racist requirements spelt out in Paper 30 (Annex 5) which came into being in 1991, under the guidance of CCETSW's Black Perspectives Committee. By 1994, the challenges against Paper 30, emanating from within the academy (see Pinker, 1993), the government (Cervi and Clark, 1993; King, 1993; *Community Care*, 1993) and the media

(Phillips, 1993; Dunant, 1994) resulted in a restructuring of CCETSW's organisational framework, the abolition of the Black Perspectives Committee, the replacement of an academic as Chair of CCETSW's governing board by a lawyer, and a Review of Paper 30. Responding to an intensive media campaign against anti-racist social work training in the summer of 1993, and under pressure from the government to 'get CCETSW's house in order', the non-academic Chair expressed serious disagreement with key elements of CCETSW's anti-racist policy because it 'alienated people' by being 'extreme' and 'going over the top' (Francis, 1994, p. 19). Despite the media hype, an overview of anti-racism training and practice before the creation of the Northern Curriculum Development Project in 1988 and prior to the introduction of the DipSW concluded that it was 'superficial, patchy and ad-hoc' (Patel, 1991, p. 12).

This evaluation had been confirmed in other research. Davies and Wright (1989) reported that 61 per cent of their respondents considered 'race awareness' as either minor or marginal on their courses. A further 13 per cent said it had been absent altogether. This contrasts with the emphasis given to other subject areas such as social policy, sociology and psychology, which had been covered by at least 79 per cent of respondents. Moreover, in identifying skills acquired during the course, only 2 per cent of trainees claimed 'race awareness'. Even this overstates the actual situation, because responses in this miscellaneous category included 'escaping from college unnoticed' and 'surviving on £35 per week'. Moreover, none of the respondents who had been in probation officer posts for at least one year mentioned anti-racist practice as an important task at work.

The Coleman Report in 1988 had also offered a depressing perspective on anti-racist course content. Coleman claimed that: 'All courses had developed or were developing courses and workshops addressing the problems of social work in a multi-racial society' (Coleman, 1988, p. 16). However, he revealed that the anti-racist course content was still under development, and that the content and style of the anti-racist input that existed 'differed widely'. Definitions of what constituted 'best practice' were unclear, and opinions appeared to 'change and differ strongly' (Coleman, 1988, p. 16).

Coleman was amongst the first to predict a backlash against anti-racist social work education. Clearly unhappy with some of the more politicised course content, he observed that anti-racism training is more 'assertive than is normal on academic courses' and 'more concerned with "consciousness raising" and indoctrination than with objective analysis of problems' (Coleman, 1988, p. 16). The Coleman Report resulted in a major reshuffle of resources on Home Office-sponsored probation courses. Meanwhile, the government claimed that courses were not being evaluated on their anti-racist course content, although courses wishing to retain Home Office funding experienced the pressures of having to take account of the government's view of 'politicised' courses.

Overall, the evidence revealed a lack of consistency and direction, a finding that CCETSW's own follow-up study in 1991 endorsed. Indeed, the situation was so chaotic that CCETSW has not published the material gathered by social work education advisers as they conducted their normal visits during that year (Patel, 1991). The need for change, if services were to match the aspirations of all people living in the multi-cultural UK was unambiguous. Yet CCETSW's greater assertiveness on this front was strongly resisted. Part of this hostile reaction was predictable. Some academics construed CCETSW's increased propensity to be prescriptive as an infringement of academic freedom. Others bemoaned the already crowded curriculum. All pointed to the lack of training skills or commitment in implementing the required changes (Morris, 1989; Ahmed, 1991).

By early 1995, opposition had been such that the movement of probation students out of DipSW training was being seriously considered. The Home Secretary suggested that a form of in-service training could be more vocationally relevant. This heralds the view that training should look less at attitudes and politics and more at tasks. We would argue that public reaction to CCETSW's stance on anti-racism has proven problematic because the thinking runs contrary to the political ideology of the New Right, which seeks to blame black people for their predicament rather than examine the structural inequalities that pervade the organisation of UK society.

Moreover, we would claim that not taking an anti-racist stance is also political. Those who maintain that UK society is not racist rely on politics which endorse an unchallenged acceptance of the status quo. These neither probe society's underlying dynamics nor seek to explain the absence of black people from positions of power and authority and the lack of welfare services to meet their needs. It also ignores substantial research evidence which indicates black people do not have their fair share of society's resources at their disposal, and disregards the daily experience of black people themselves (see Brown, 1984; Smith, 1976; Bhat et al., 1988; Wilson, 1977; ADSS, 1978; Taylor, 1981; Swann, 1985; Eggleston, 1987).

Anti-racist training and practice which accept the existence of institutional racism and oppression are:

> uncongenial to the politics of 'race relations' which portrays Britain as an essentially 'open and tolerant society troubled by a minority of individual racists'. (Husband, 1991, p. 54)

The notion of UK society as tolerant is a recurring theme in this debate. This point has been emphasised by the CCETSW chair, who explained that Paper 30 alienated 'right-thinking members of society, tolerant, decent people' (Francis, 1994, p. 19).

Tolerance has two meanings: to recognise others' beliefs or lifestyles without sharing them; or to put up with these reluctantly. To deny the endemic nature of racism in UK society and focus on the perceived tolerance of decent folk trivialises the reality of black people's experience. Moreover, the UK's claims to tolerance are by no means unambiguous.

Many groups who define themselves as 'decent people' experience oppression, and struggle to become beneficiaries of this 'tolerant society'. They are excluded from enjoying full citizenship rights and participating in society through various forms of oppression. Social workers and probation officers work mainly with those that society excludes for a variety of reasons: punishment; the excluded person's 'own good'; age; illness; behaviour society does not understand or approve of, and differences in lifestyles.

An understanding of the politics of exclusion, the connections between structural inequalities and individual circumstances, is critical if social workers are to intervene effectively in people's daily lives. Practitioners lacking the knowledge base linked to this understanding and unable to use this in practical ways in their work with people can only offer a poor service. That is why learning about black people and applying this knowledge in practice must remain central to the training process in both the academy and the field.

Sadly, focusing on tolerance is misguided – tolerance does not give oppressed people rights and equality of opportunity. Tolerance is finite and always contains the implied threat of danger when tolerance runs out. It gives excluded people only a period of grace while their behaviour is on probation. The questions remain: 'Will they or will they not be accepted?'; 'For how long?'

Anti-racist social work, whether carried out in college or on the employers' premises, provides students with the conceptual tools which help them to make sense of the complex political realities which we have identified above, as well as equipping them with the practical skills for working with people in less oppressive ways. That is why anti-racist social work is an absolutely essential part of training. It can only be ignored if the practitioner is willing to lower his or her standards of practice. However, anti-racist social work's capacity to challenge inadequate practice has made it vulnerable to attack by those who prefer individualised and pathological explanations of social problems. Hence the charge that anti-racist social work is about doctrinaire pandering to 'political correctness' (see Dunnant, 1994).

Dominelli (1992) argues that such accusations aim to discredit and trivialise voices and opinions raised in opposition to New Right thinking, and have a clear political agenda:

> This attack on those being accused of dogmatism through their 'political correctness' is being launched to distract attention from the messages they are delivering

because the messages are uncomfortable ones which shake our cherished percep-
tions of ourselves as tolerant and fair people (individually and collectively) and
because some powerful people have invested much in maintaining inequality in
order to benefit from it. (Dominelli, 1992, p. 58)

The unwillingness of government, and others in powerful positions within
agencies and in social work education, to fully acknowledge the existence of
cultural and institutional racism or grapple with the ways in which a tolerant
society oppresses certain categories of people leaves anti-racist and anti-
oppressive practice vulnerable to the swings of governmental and media
opinion. Moreover, their stance has meant that CCETSW's anti-racist practice initiative, developed in response to practitioners' and academics' cries
for help in progressing the realisation of anti-racist social work (Patel, 1994,
p. 7), had been significantly undermined within three years of its inception.
As a result, there is the potential loss of any consistency gained through
DipSW, and the return to the chaotic approaches that typified course content
prior to its introduction. Such an outcome would greatly disadvantage practitioners and service users.

Thus we conclude that, far from 'going over the top', white practitioners
have only made a start in understanding and rejecting racism. Further
growth in this area requires working co-operatively with other people who
share their aspirations in exploring some of their deepest emotions before
taking action which will create a more egalitarian world for all. To move this
work forward, white workers must support rather than compete with each
other.

In-service training: Problems and possibilities

An essential role for training and development staff is that of promoting the
understanding of anti-racist practice relevant to white 'clients' and users.
That misconceptions abound was evidenced in Holdaway and Allaker's
(1990, p. 9) research, in which one Probation Service claimed that 'race' was
'not a problem in our area'. Such responses reflect misconceived views about
anti-racist practice on both DipSW and in-service training courses.

Worker–worker relationships

The lack of consistent training on qualifying courses creates problems for
in-service trainers, who have to respond to the diverse training needs of
qualified staff. Some practitioners feel that the different forms of training
they have received during their social work careers can provide them with

an overall understanding of the issue. But for many, the often unexplained changes in language and emphasis have proved intimidating.

The experience of inconsistent training, the enormous variety in the ways in which anti-racist statements have been applied in practice and the political and media debate about it, can make it difficult for anti-racist practitioners to grow in confidence and develop their practice.

Attempts to provide quality training amidst this uncertainty can only be of limited effect. Although these are far from ideal circumstances, what are some of the issues relating to in-service training that practitioners and trainers face, and what may be ways forward?

We have identified the key areas which in-service trainers must address when planning their courses as follows:

- different starting points amongst participants;
- participants' reluctance to expose their prior knowledge of the issues;
- newness;
- 'broad-brush' approaches to basic training;
- group mix and dynamics.

These five items involve organisational policies and procedures, inter-personal interactions and individual expectations. Considering their implications for training courses – whether at pre-qualifying, or post-qualifying level – will improve both course content and group dynamics.

Different starting points

Having identified the great diversity in trainees' experience and understanding of anti-racism as a persistent problem in planning appropriate training, in-service trainers cannot assume a 'baseline' of knowledge amongst course participants. Their heterogeneous starting points, particularly if pre-qualifying and post-qualifying officers are involved in any given course, must provide the foundation for their work together. Otherwise, the group processes will hinder rather than aid learning.

Practice Example

At a multi-agency training event on the inclusion of families in case conferences, the majority of those present described themselves as 'multi-cultural-ists'. Their expectation was to be given generalised information about how families from different black communities functioned. When this was not provided, the atmosphere of the event changed. Participants claimed it was a 'waste of time' and the trainers were subject to some hostility.

Clarity about the aims and objectives of this training event would have facilitated the learning process.

White workers' sensitivity in addressing racism has acquired the status of a truism. Trainers can respond to these concerns by meticulously choosing the materials for sessions, introducing ground rules and being careful in their delivery of the course. However, as long as such initiatives challenge well-established views, emotions and behaviours about racism which white people find hard to admit, anti-racist activities will retain their 'difficult' label. To some extent, this state of affairs is a self-fulfilling prophecy. White people's beliefs that encountering problems in anti-racist training is the norm mean that suggestions to the contrary are greeted with incredulity. Yet our experiences indicate that, whilst anti-racist work is challenging, thought-provoking and at times frightening, it can also be enlightening, enjoyable, informative and full of the promise of change. It can also enhance the quality of life and be very funny.

Trainers who fail to emphasise the positives for participants can unwittingly promote a climate of gloom. Anti-racism training can also be made more complicated if the subject is misrepresented by being portrayed as attitudinally neutral. Occasionally, an economic, class-based critique is introduced to extend course coverage, but it is still retained within non-threatening parameters for white participants. We would argue that it is important for trainers to conduct a dialogue about the 'politics of training' with their students. Such discussions would enable course participants to share their concerns more honestly.

Finally, anti-racism is difficult because white workers fear 'getting it wrong' or 'saying the wrong thing'. When describing the role of a non-disabled ally, Michelene Mason of the Disability Movement gives easy-to-follow, practical advice for moving forward from this position. We feel her message is also relevant for anti-racists. She writes, we need allies:

> not to be 'experts' or managers of our lives ... we need you to admit cheerfully what you don't know, without shame; to ask us what we need before providing it. (Mason, 1992, p. 78)

Part of white workers' insecurity stems from the lack of support from other white workers. Trainers can help connect anti-racist individuals with each other so that they can overcome their isolation and work together as allies. Sadly, some white workers have abused their knowledge of anti-racism through power games aimed at belittling colleagues. Such action betrays the spirit of anti-racism, which is rooted in a personal politics which seeks to create the conditions in which self-empowerment and liberation can take place. It is not about a set of attitudes to be showed off in the right – or 'right on' – company.

Exposing one's prior knowledge of the issues

The trainer's assessment of course participants' prior knowledge of anti-racist social work is further complicated by white students' and practitioners' reluctance to admit what they 'know' about the subject. The fear of exposing their vulnerabilities generates anxieties which block their ability to share their views and opinions frankly with each other. In the presence of their peers, anti-racism becomes a topic about which they must neither know too much nor too little. Proceeding along these lines means that students and practitioners are unable to evaluate their own anti-racist knowledge before the course and may miss the opportunity to explore the issue and enhance their knowledge of anti-racism. Trainers who enable participants to discuss their fears openly have a greater chance of promoting 'real' learning amongst the course group.

Practice Example

> *Prior to a team-based training event, team members indicated a general lack of knowledge and confidence about anti-racism. Afterwards, although the training was generally well received, feedback comments included: 'material was familiar from former training', 'would have been more useful if I had not done a two-and-a-half-day training event recently' and 'the issue is exhausted'.*

If course participants could have articulated their specific training needs earlier, this opportunity for training could have been used more effectively and provided a more enriching experience for them.

Newness

Following qualification, probation officers begin their appointments as 'newcomers'. The 'new officer' is put 'on probation' and closely assessed for competence on a protected caseload before 'confirmation'. Increasingly, services are insisting on compulsory training for 'new' officers with less than two years' post-qualification experience. Being viewed as 'new' discourages the public acknowledgement of prior anti-racism training. It may also prevent newer staff from commenting on the poor practice they see around them. Newly-qualified staff with a commitment to anti-racist practice may find that they are tolerated by colleagues with the expectation they will soon run out of steam and become better assimilated into the prevailing custom and practice.

Practice Example

> *One worker received some type of anti-racism training in three different*

Probation Services; had further anti-racist training on his CQSW course; participated in anti-racist training for colleagues and volunteers, and, in his third year as a 'new' officer, went through the Probation Service's basic introductory anti-racism training programme. He had valued the chance to update his knowledge, and the later training helped him to understand why he had found the initial 'Racism Awareness Training' so disturbing. However, his overall experience had been confusing, as no attempt had been made to integrate these different experiences.

This worker needed time and support to seek common threads in his training and consolidate his experiences. Being able to take advantage of such opportunities would have enabled him to plan a developmental approach to anti-racist social work and reduce the feeling that he was not getting anywhere because he was always starting from scratch.

'Broad-brush' basic training

The report of the Race Issues Advisory Committee for the National Association for the Care and Resettlement of Offenders (NACRO, 1993a) reviewed research on anti-racist training. It observed that probation areas have focused their staff training on 'race awareness', thereby failing to connect with practice. As a result, trainers shifted to anti-racist practice training. Yet Probation Services continue to require all current and new staff to receive a 'broad-brush introductory training' on the subject. This 'broad-brush training' falls somewhere between 'race awareness' and anti-racist practice. The product of this mix is perhaps inevitably disappointing, because it reflects lack of clarity about training objectives and its scope. Moreover, it occurs too infrequently for material to be adequately followed up.

'Broad-brush basic training' for anti-racist social work becomes problematic as training budgets become squeezed through cash limits and questions are raised about 'squandering' precious resources on basic training which qualified staff should have obtained on their social work courses.

'Broad-brush basic training' also raises the issue of compulsory training – a concept that has generated controversy amongst probation officers who believe in practising as autonomous professionals. Yet exercising their discretion has led to anomalies in which officers who refuse to attend 'Anti-Racism Training' on principle, because it is compulsory, quickly jettison these principles when instructed to attend training on successive Criminal Justice Acts.

Practice Example

The anti-racism training received by white staff in one probation district started with definitions of racism, work on 'race awareness' including basic stereotyping exercises. The course also attempted to consider practice. However, as the course participants were derived from different teams, identifying common practice examples became problematic. The matter was further complicated by the trainer's insistence that the practice area chosen be video-taped. Group members responded by thinking not about areas of practice that caused them real concern, but about what would fit the video. The trainers did well to hold together the range of material presented by such a diverse group. But the question of what had been achieved remained. One cynical conclusion was that another group 'had been processed'.

Trying to develop one training course appropriate to the needs of an entire Probation Service with different levels of experience, skills, knowledge, qualifications and commitment to the subject is virtually impossible. Despite the major resource implications of whole-district training, this form of training does not represent a real commitment to anti-racism by management. Too frequently the training is isolated from practice, and other Home Office or management initiatives which could foster anti-racist practice training are ignored.

Group mix and dynamics

The composition of a course group affects the dynamics within which learning takes place. Its make-up needs careful consideration if group dynamics are to be channelled in ways which assist the learning process. Group heterogeneity, for example, can have an impact on how comfortable people feel in exposing their vulnerabilities on a contentious subject such as anti-racist social work. Thus trainers will have to ensure that the purposes of the course match those of the group. If its members share common objectives and/or attributes, they are more likely to work effectively together. If group matching conflicts with management's aim of containing training costs by having the service train together, trainers will have to think of how to subdivide people into smaller groups to examine those aspects of the course which are better handled by people with similar characteristics working together, as well as providing space in which all course participants work as a whole group.

Employer–employee relationships: Managing anti-racist work in mixed teams

Training of black and white staff: Together or separately?

This chapter focuses largely on anti-racist training for white practitioners and students, but it is also important to consider the role and training needs of black staff and students. There is no consensus on whether black and white practitioners should receive anti-racism training in mixed groups. The main reason for this is that, if racism is white people's problem, their training should highlight how they can eliminate their own racism, whilst black practitioners need black affirmation training to equip them with strategies for coping with the racism they encounter within the criminal justice system.

Ultimately, however, we believe that training should equip both black and white practitioners to work together, thereby initiating anti-racist social work at operational level. With this in mind, we argue that employers have a key role to play in creating a working environment that fosters egalitarian relations between both black and white workers and providing their workers with training opportunities which enable them to develop such relationships (they will not happen automatically). In implementing such a policy, employers will have to ensure that both black and white staff have the space to work autonomously on their own specific needs, as well as together – a point which we consider in greater detail below.

In Chapter 3 we illustrated how effective teamwork can be when challenging racism in the workplace. The following Practice Example illustrates how working together can also create dilemmas for management and trainers who have to meet the needs of different group members and deal with uncomfortable feelings. These matters need to be recognised and addressed.

Practice Example

One service made attendance on an anti-racism course optional for black workers. They were, however, expected to go on a black affirmation course. One black officer elected to go on anti-racism training with his white colleagues. He made this choice because he felt it was important for him to attend the training to contribute to the team's anti-racism strategy and learn about his white colleagues' starting points on anti-racist practice. The remaining black workers went on the black affirmation course. During the first day on the anti-racism course, there was no reference to black perspectives by either trainers or trainees. At the end of the day, the black member asked his white colleagues how they felt about his presence on the course. They replied that they felt embarrassed and guilty discussing their feelings before him, and experienced his question as very liberating. The following day, the atmosphere on the course was very different as white colleagues began to openly discuss the issues.

This Practice Example raises a number of difficult points. The poor quality of training initially meant that participants colluded with the racism present in the training process until the black officer challenged it. The dynamics confirm that many white practitioners remain uncomfortable discussing racism. This can create barriers to the development of meaningful alliances between black and white colleagues. The actions of the black member enhanced the quality of training by exposing hidden agendas and challenging all course members to own the training objectives.

However, it is not the responsibility of black staff to liberate white colleagues. In this Practice Example, trainers should have ensured that black perspectives were incorporated into the course, thereby helping white individuals liberate themselves without putting black participants on the spot. It also highlights the need for black affirmation courses to equip black staff to identify ways of addressing their own needs and acquire skills in handling racist situations. In other words, both anti-racist and black affirmation courses ought to be made available to black staff.

Yet we are aware that budgetary constraints have led services to limit training for black staff to one type of course or the other. This can be false economy, as both black and white staff need to be empowered to make their contribution to social change. It would have helped if the employers in the Practice Example above had provided the resources necessary for both black and white staff to have training opportunities in same-'race' groups, and subsequently to undertake anti-racist social work training in a mixed group. Such a course of action would have enabled each same-'race' group to identify and address their own particular training needs, and once these had been tackled, go on to focus on how black and white workers could work effectively in egalitarian relationships with each other. The problem of white people dumping responsibility for their own growth and learning on black people could have thus been avoided.

Training across the 'racial divide'

Besides establishing an appropriate environment for participants to explore their fears, vulnerabilities and strengths, other matters require careful thought before training sessions are launched. One of these is to ensure that individuals do not leave the course feeling that they must single-handedly tackle the whole of the racist edifice which they both repudiate and endorse in their daily interactions. Another is enabling individual participants to influence the process whereby learning takes place. Having a modicum of control over their learning environment and owning the programme through which their personal growth proceeds makes it easier for individuals to take responsibility for becoming anti-racist practitioners.

A further message that needs affirming is that *personal* racism is only *one* form of racism. There are others – institutional and cultural racism, which feed into and out of it. These too must be addressed specifically. Course members should also be encouraged to think of how they might get together with others to feel less overwhelmed by the enormity of the task which faces them (see Dominelli, 1994; Powell and Edmonds, 1985).

Working with others who appreciate one's points of view, life experience and ability to engage with the issue of racism needs validating for both white and black course participants. This may mean making available the resources, trainers, space and materials for black students to work with black trainers in autonomous black groups. Autonomous black groups should not be confused with separatist black groups. The former are essential in facilitating the development of black perspectives and agendas which promote the growth of black support groups and demand changes in the social relationships which give rise to racism. Autonomous black groups also provide black people with the opportunity to be with others like themselves – an opportunity which white people take for granted. Separatist groups are more focused on developing a black society which parallels the mainstream white one. White people find separatist groups much more threatening. They fear that black separatist groups will end up turning the tables on them, and that in taking control of social resources usually denied them by white people, their actions will lead to the material impoverishment of white people.

Black affirmation courses in the Probation Service provide black workers with the opportunity to meet with each other and to share their experiences of working within the criminal justice system. An important aspect of affirmation is the 'feelgood factor' which develops when workers are able to celebrate the diversity of their struggles and survival in environments which often equate 'black' with being 'bad'. Black affirmation courses aim to empower black people to feel positive about being black, despite the negativity towards them emanating from powerful institutions – education, State religion, employment, the criminal justice system and media.

These institutions are powerful shapers of the ways in which black people see themselves and each other. The acceptance of the negative valuations these institutions ascribe to black people must be challenged if black people are to take control of their lives and set the parameters within which their interaction with white people take place. The following Practice Example illustrates this point.

Practice Example

During the morning of the first day of a three-day affirmation course for black members of staff, the facilitators suggested that it would be good for all the participants to go out for a meal at the end of the course. This was agreed in principle, and the next step was to decide where to go. At this stage, one of the black members of staff stated a preference for going to a place which did not serve foreign food.

This request caused a degree of consternation within the group. Facilitators and course members had to 'unpack' this before feeling able to celebrate the differences in culture and perspectives contributed by black employees.

This example demonstrates the importance of black people gaining the space within which to make their own demands and have these taken seriously. It also indicates how anti-racist training also needs to enable black workers and 'clients' to understand the ways in which racism shapes the interaction which takes place between them as black people.

Our work has revealed that the practicalities of running sessions on anti-racist training are influenced by the composition of the group, individuals' knowledge levels and the length of their experience as probation workers. Thus we recommend ample opportunity for course participants to speak to each other in various combinations and in groups of various sizes. Careful thought should be given to when students should work in plenary format and when in small groups. *The processes which take place in these sessions are as important as the content of the curriculum.*

We would argue that raising people's consciousness of racism and the complex dynamics through which it operates is a fairly time-consuming and resource-intensive process which cannot be short-circuited. Yet our experiences of working in resource-starved public institutions is that this kind of work is amongst the first 'luxuries' to be cut. As a result, we have had to develop alternative ways of proceeding which are less dependent on contact between trainers and students. In making up for this resource deficit, we have drawn on technological facilities, distance learning packages, shorter periods of trainer–student contact time, and student-led groups. Whilst such approaches are useful, their appropriateness is limited. They do not make up for personal contact, nor do they provide the instantaneous feedback on both content and process which a trainer drawing on a bank of expertise can do.

We will now turn to examining some of the dilemmas and processes which we have encountered through our own work as anti-racists. The examples we have chosen to illustrate specific points are arbitrary: we could have picked any of a number. However, the issues we consider are very important.

White trainer, black student   The 'student' can be either a colleague at the same level of the organisation, higher up in the hierarchy or lower. It may also be a student on placement from a qualifying course. Each of these situations creates a different set of power dynamics, each of which must be considered in the preparation and planning of the course. Trainers may have to argue with their employers that better training opportunities can be provided if the groups are established as 'peer' groups. If this course of action cannot be followed, a discussion of power differentials and their impact on group dynamics would be useful in clearing the air. It may also be possible to subdivide the group at the points at which power differentials matter. Finally, the role of the trainers as teachers, the 'students' as students, and the mutual learning which occurs between them also need to be considered. Notwithstanding these differences, which need to be acknowledged, there are common threads which the trainers also have to address.

White trainers working with white students have a difficult time ensuring that they do not set up false expectations about what can be achieved through training. They also need to take steps that will prevent their colluding with each other and minimising the significance of racism in their own interactions with each other.

Whilst covering these matters, white anti-racist trainers working with black students will encounter a further set of dynamics which must be addressed directly. Black people's reactions to them will vary. Some will lack faith in their ability to do the work required of them. Given that much of what is expected of anti-racist trainers is an understanding of black people's position as *black* people, and few white trainers are able to offer this in practice, this is not surprising. Few white people have taken the time to immerse themselves in the rich diversity of black lifestyles and appreciate how much they have offered our society. Even fewer white people have developed sufficiently deep, egalitarian relationships with black communities to feel that they truly understand what black perspectives say about life and what these have to offer. Finally, few white people have been subjected to a daily onslaught on their personhood and integrity, and developed the skills necessary to survive in such a situation. These failings ill equip white trainers for working with black students. However, these issues must be addressed by white people, for, given the current demographic position, black students are more likely to encounter white trainers than black ones.

White trainers who work with black students need the skills to deal with their own racism, but also with both the desire for liberation and the battle against internalised racism on the part of black students. Providing an appropriate service in these circumstances is not easy, but it requires an active and well-developed relationship between white trainers and black trainers, and a willingness on the part of the white trainer to be flexible and really *listen* to what black people are saying. It also requires humility on the part of white trainers, a commitment to anti-racist practice and a willingness to own up to mistakes which they make.

Practice Example

Chris was a young UK-born woman of Chinese descent. She was bright, vivacious and outgoing. Suddenly, this changed and she developed serious behavioural problems while in her last year at school. She was referred to her local social services department, which had an equal opportunities policy. There, she was offered a Chinese-speaking social worker as part of the department's commitment to racial matching. The decision was inappropriate to begin with. Chris did not speak Chinese. However, the matter was complicated further in that Chris refused to have anything to do with this worker. The worker's passable use of English was irrelevant as far as Chris was concerned. She did not see herself as 'black', and she did not need a Chinese-speaking social worker. The department concerned then said that it could not offer her another social worker as its policy was that 'clients' who refused black workers (for implied racist reasons) would not be given a white social worker.

This case was placed on the table for discussion by a white worker carrying the case at a training event. The majority of group participants who were white felt that the social services department had acted appropriately. The white trainer challenged this view and encouraged the group participants to put themselves in Chris's position and consider the case with her actual needs in mind. This would require them to exercise their capacity for empathy, find out what Chris thought her needs were, and 'unpack' with her why she felt as she did about the black worker. In other words, a thorough assessment was called for, not a reliance on stereotypes about either UK-born blacks of Chinese descent or the meaning of anti-racist social work. The process whereby the work was done had to be at one with the principles of anti-racist practice. Since Chris had initially refused to speak with a black social worker, a recognition of her capacity to make her own decisions about her life meant that a black worker could not be imposed upon her. She would need to reverse her position herself. Others could only contribute to an educational process which left her with open options which she could explore.

However, given that the white trainer suspected that internalised racism was an important factor in Chris's decision, it seemed appropriate for the white social worker to consult closely with black social workers about how to proceed in her discussions with her. These attempted to examine Chris's feelings about herself, her own identity and self-esteem. A focus on her views about black people was to come much later, when progress had been made on this front. Over the months, with the trainer supporting the white worker in question, and the two of them constantly reviewing the progress she was making on the case with black social workers, Chris's poor view of black people and of herself 'as something other than a white person' came out. This was then addressed directly for some time before she made a request for a black worker herself. Chris was subsequently able to work effectively with a black social worker who assumed the case.

Dealing with internalised racism is not a matter of dogmatic assertions. In Chris's case, the social workers' (both black and white) efforts were hampered by the department's insistence on following 'procedure' even when it made little sense. Much of the social workers' time was spent fighting the organisation which should have been supporting their efforts, not undermining them. The social workers could have done without such interference. It is to their credit that they were able to transcend this and work effectively together to provide the services which Chris needed.

This case highlights the importance of black and white social workers working in partnership with each other if they are to deal effectively with the complexities of racism, undo the damage racism has caused black people, improve services to 'clients' and ameliorate their practice. Furthermore, it indicates how easy it is for managers who are unaware of the complexities of anti-racist social work to obstruct changes to their policies, despite their intentions to the contrary, and for organisations to ignore their institutional racism (the lack of black employees), thereby providing a poorer service to black and white 'clients'. It also provides a model whereby trainers and fieldworkers can work effectively with each other and draw on the expertise of black colleagues without holding them responsible for whatever progress is made on a case.

Practice Example

A young, white social work lecturer was asked to run a tutorial group which included UK-born people of Afro-Caribbean descent, UK-born people of Asian descent, people born in the Indian subcontinent, students who came from China and several white students of English descent born in the UK. The students followed a variety of religions – Christian, Muslim, Sikh and Hindu. For a while, the white lecturer, who considered herself an anti-racist, struggled alone to bring in different perspectives, an appreciation of people coming from different positions to oneself and an opportunity to make demands of the group necessary for their own personal education. Although the discussions were interesting and the students as a whole claimed they got a lot out of the group, she felt unable to meet the expectations she had of herself.

Feeling she needed to get help and support from outside the department she worked in, as it was not forthcoming from that quarter, she went and asked a black trainer with strong roots in various black communities to help her. Outlining her strategy to get her department to commit resources to buy in several black practitioners who could support autonomous black support groups for black students, she asked her black colleague to assist her in identifying black practitioners who might have the requisite skills and who could be approached to do the work. She also shared with her black colleague her concern about using black people to do casual, sessional teaching. She did not feel that she could pursue full-time posts as there had been no such appointments in her department for several years. Her black colleague reassured her that it was more important to get black practitioners in to do a specific task which met the identified needs of black students than to worry about changing institutional practices at that point in time. Feeling empowered by her contact with her black colleague and much more confident about her proposed plans, she thanked her black colleague for her support and went back to her tutorial group.

This Practice Example indicates how easy it is for educational institutions to ignore their institutional racism (the lack of black employees) and provide a poorer service to students as a result. It also shows how white anti-racists are drawn into colluding with the racist practices brought about by the lack of appropriate resources, and demonstrates the importance of black and white trainers working together to improve both services to students and the practice that ensues. Another salutary point brought out in the case materials is the importance of realising that, whilst changing individual practices requires institutional change to take place, it is not necessary for the same person to feel responsible for intervening at all these levels simultaneously.

Proposed model for in-service anti-racist practice training

Staff in the training and development section of a Probation Service must take a more central role in in-service training if it is to be more fully integrated with practice. Achieving this objective also requires probation management to develop its own anti-racist practice, and for them to take seriously how the organisation can provide an environment which fosters anti-racist social work as a routine part of employees' working conditions.

Anti-racist practice is currently formally absent from training planning, staff appraisal procedures and supervision plans whilst being deemed central in the 'client'–worker relationship. Senior managers can play a crucial role in addressing this issue by encouraging closer co-operation between staff from the training and development section and officers responsible for supervising staff. Working together, these groups could bring anti-racist practice more into the mainstream of probation work, consult with operational staff and identify issues that need attention at the organisational, team and individual levels.

The limited culture of anti-racism in the Probation Service means that the quality of supervision a probation officer with a commitment to anti-racist practice receives relies heavily on luck as to which senior they get and how much that senior knows or cares about anti-racist social work. Planning supervision and training from an anti-racist perspective for supervisors could end such haphazardness. It would also enable attention to be devoted to improving the organisational culture for anti-racist social work. Some of the impetus for moving forward on this front could call upon the relevant proposals of the Grimsey Scrutiny of in-service probation training launched from the Cabinet Office in the early 1990s (see Hadjipavlou and Murphy, 1991).

Training planning

The managerial imperative of controlling costs has compelled Probation Services to become more disciplined in allocating training opportunities to workers. Until recently, main grade probation officers went on whatever training they fancied. Limited attention was paid to its relevance to either an individual's personal or the team's training needs. Training was taken by many as a break from the tedium of work. Whilst using training as a reward may be legitimate, such an approach has neither helped to identify workers' training needs nor facilitated monitoring of whether these have been met.

Creating a training portfolio for each worker which includes anti-racism training as a distinct requirement should become a regular part of supervision. By identifying an individual's experience and training throughout their working life, training opportunities can be more appropriately tailored to meet needs. Equally, such exercises can enable managers to recognise more effectively skills and strengths that could be channelled towards meeting the needs of others. Consulting with all the relevant staff involved in developing and delivering training makes it easier to find responses which will most appropriately meet identified needs. These could include: a course; team-based training; access to literature, videos or other resources, and introductions to other workers with the relevant knowledge and skills.

This last suggestion may be viewed with suspicion for merely cutting the costs of training, and runs a risk of being abused. The history of anti-racism is replete with examples of white workers using black workers as experts by dumping responsibility for securing anti-racist changes on them. However, many probation workers claim to have learnt far more from colleagues than from any other source. Used carefully, the skills of black and white men and women colleagues are of great value in a training context. In reality, many workers network informally to meet their own training needs. Planning can regularise such contacts and extend them to those currently excluded by informal mechanisms. Moreover, formalising the process via supervision makes both manager and worker accountable for the work being done, recorded and acted upon.

Training or development needs can be met either formally or informally.

The following Practice Example illustrates how people informally provide training for each other.

Practice Example

One white worker was struggling with aspects of his own reaction to black young men in the street. Whilst always wary of groups of white young men, he was even more wary of black young men. This did not fit with his personal experience of being assaulted or involved in fights with white, but not black youths, when he was younger. A conversation with a white colleague who had a similar experience was of help. It was easy to identify the role of newspapers, with their presentation of black men as potentially violent. But their discussion went further, to examine a shared experience of cultural racism. During their upbringing, white people were usually referred to as individuals, whereas black people were portrayed as 'all the same' except for a few 'honoured' exceptions. The colleague identified two resources he had found useful: the video Being White *and the book* Staying Power *(Fryer, 1984). This low-key intervention was greatly valued by the first worker.*

Such support should be both recognised and encouraged.

Staff appraisal

Staff appraisal has been formally incorporated into the supervision of probation staff. The appraisal forms in use for main grade officers make no reference to anti-racist or even anti-discriminatory practice. If individual workers want to be appraised on their anti-racist practice, they must actively request that this be set as an 'objective'. The suspicion surrounding this method of appraisal means few individual staff are likely to raise such requests. However, staff from the training and development section could argue the necessity of appraising workers on their anti-racist practice. Probation Services rejecting such calls could have their commitment to anti-racist practice and the resourcing of basic training in it publicly questioned.

A positive appraisal of anti-racist practice would help keep it central to daily practice, assist in the accurate identification of further training needs and highlight examples of good practice which could be shared with the training and development staff to form a good practice reference point. Good practice could be exchanged between training staff and field colleagues, used specifically to respond to enquiries about developments in anti-racist practice, and advertised.

Practice Example

A Social Enquiry Report written by a student on placement was noted by a senior probation officer as being an example of good anti-racist practice. The SER was subsequently used by practice teachers in seminars on report writing for students for the next few years, adapted somewhat on the introduction of Pre-Sentence Reports.

Maintaining a data bank of good practice in the training department could ensure that no individual piece of work was over-used, and could publicise examples of good work which was being undertaken by individuals, teams and the organisation.

Supervision plans

National Standards dictate that Supervision Plans specify the work that a probation officer intends to do with a 'client' on a Probation Order. One positive feature of a Supervision Plan is the involvement of the 'client' in its production. Supervision Plans are central to work undertaken with 'clients' and provide the basis for monitoring progress; the documentation is presented as 'race'- and gender-neutral. Thus, whilst the detailed format and content of Supervision Plans vary around the country, none of those we have examined include reference to anti-racist or anti-discriminatory work as an item for the officer and 'client' to address when they meet.

We wonder how anti-racism training can be allegedly important in practice if it is absent from such a key document. Practitioners, their seniors and staff from the training and development section could raise this omission as a matter for rectification with senior management. One could, for example, include a section on the Supervision Plan pro-forma which asks the officer and 'client' to identify anti-racist or anti-discriminatory issues relevant to supervision and their work plans. Learning how to make positive use of such a section could become an area covered during training. At the very least, Supervision Plans could record that the 'client' has been informed of the anti-racist policy of the agency and the procedures that would be invoked in the agency's response to anyone displaying racist and offensive language or behaviour.

Clearly, these issues can stretch under-resourced and marginalised in-service training departments. Senior managers therefore need to ensure that the necessary resources are forthcoming, and that line management structures and procedures work effectively to implement policies which incorporate measures on anti-oppressive practice in Supervision Plans.

Practice Example

National Standards have required probation staff to be much clearer in explaining the requirements of supervision to 'clients'. However, there is no instruction to consider other important issues that will affect their experience of supervision. One northern district runs an information session for new or returning 'clients'. In addition to the 'legal' requirements of supervision, three other significant points are raised with all 'clients' who attend. These are:

i   The anti-racist policy of the agency, *that is, how the agency will respond to racist language and behaviour and how 'clients' should expect probation staff to treat them during contact, including that which may arise with family and friends of the 'client'.*

ii   The child protection role of the service *and what that may mean in practice should a worker have concerns about the welfare of any child they come into contact with during supervision. This is, in many workers' opinion, the best-kept secret of being on probation/supervision, unless the 'client' is a Schedule 1 offender.*

iii   The complaints procedure and process *are explained and the relevant senior probation officer for handling possible complaints is identified. 'Clients' are encouraged to use the system if they experience racism, other forms of discrimination or feel they are treated unfairly. 'Clients' are also asked to use the same system if they feel they have been treated positively by the Probation Service.*

Training which is isolated from practice is unlikely to have a lasting influence. One-off training events do not change the culture of organisations, no matter how well they are delivered. Anti-racist practice and training requires organisational change. Without such change, trainers face an impossible task and are open to criticism from all directions:

> training can be viewed as a panacea – it is expected to achieve something without the necessary changes being made overall. It is bound to lead to disappointment, or to tokenism: a feeling that if staff have 'done the training' then no more action is required. (NACRO, 1993, p. 21)

We believe that concentrating the trainers' role on the staff in the training and development section provides an opportunity to influence the structure and culture of the agency more widely. Encouraging in-service trainers to adopt a model in which they assume a developmental and consultative role also highlights the importance of developing anti-racist practice with white people.

Team-based training

Anti-racist practice needs to be understood in relation to white 'clients' and workers, as well as the creation of appropriate services for black people.

Anti-racist social work should be central to training planning, staff appraisal and supervision plans. In-service training departments could adopt developmental and consultative roles in assisting teams to identify specific training needs and provisions. Developing these themes could enable in-service trainers to offer varied training relevant to meeting needs that teams have identified. Training which reflects anti-racist principles also addresses questions about the venue and whether black and white workers should train in the same groups.

In responding to these issues, an understanding of anti-racist practice appropriate to working with white 'clients' is essential. If training is team-based, and the team has black and white workers, training together to meet an agreed need may be entirely appropriate. However, if the team aims to develop its anti-racist practice with white 'clients', it should not be assumed that black workers will wish to be involved. Indeed, we would argue that it is the responsibility of white workers to address their own racism and that of white 'clients', drawing on their black colleagues' expertise primarily to check out their plans.

The specific consideration of anti-racist practice by every team could ensure that each location and building could offer an 'anti-racist' environment and stand as possible venues. However, doing so would require that white workers put effort into creating similar facilities to those existing in black voluntary organisations in mainstream workplaces. This would allow for a lesser reliance on statutory agencies' capacity to exploit black community resources by drawing on their credibility as anti-racist venues.

Practice Example

After basic anti-racism training, one team was asked to produce an anti-racist practice statement. This was written on the provision of services to black 'clients', despite there being no black 'clients' for the team to work with. The statement also ignored the need to change the environment inside and outside the building. Three years later, after new members had joined the team, a new practice statement relevant to working in a white community was produced by pooling the thoughts of all team members. One of its central features focused on the building itself. Whilst black people's absence amongst either 'clients' or staff was considered, positive images of black people were incorporated in the decor of the building. In addition, concerns about black people's experiences in such offices were to be raised during contact with 'clients'. The team would have welcomed the provision of a consultant provided by the training department to support them in their efforts and assist them in addressing racism amongst white people. For the team had uncovered many examples of practice statements for working with black people, but none for working with white people.

Managers must ensure that white workers move beyond the stage of *only* looking at service delivery to black people to consider also what work needs to be undertaken by white people for and with themselves.

'Client'–worker relationships

Anti-racist practice with white 'clients'

Anti-racist social work affirms and values difference, rather than equating it with deficit. It also places the spotlight on how power is used to control and oppress people by limiting their opportunities for self-development:

> Social work redefined according to anti-racist criteria is not about control but about realising significant improvements in the life chances and well being of individuals regardless of their gender, race, class, age, physical or intellectual abilities, sexual orientation, religious affiliation or linguistic capabilities. (Dominelli, 1988, p. 16)

If social workers and probation officers orient their energies to empowering 'clients' rather than controlling them according to stereotype, anti-racist social work becomes easier to achieve.

Moreover, anti-racist practice focuses on understanding that economic exclusion is not the only way society oppresses, and recognises that there are as many differences as similarities amongst peoples. In short, difference portrays a diverse reality against mythological 'normality' and sameness.

With regard to family structures, workers in the Probation Service engage with a variety of people and are privileged in knowing about the wide range of 'family' experiences amongst the population they work with. People may be separated or divorced; have experienced parent or child mortality; have been adopted or fostered; live with a single parent, same-sex parents, grandparents or older sibling(s); be 'new' families with new relationships; be cared for by families with disabled parents or children; be part of a family which has a parent or child with learning difficulties; be the child of infertile parents, or survive within abusive relationships. Each of these structures calls upon people to develop coping strategies which enable them to survive. Thus practitioners need to assess the strengths of such diverse family settings, and not look only for weaknesses.

Probation workers who collude with assumptions that define 'difference' as problematic rather than engaging in a specific assessment of any given situation, will stand little chance of realising significant improvements in the life circumstances of people different from themselves. Workers who accept dishonest and stereotyped representations of 'normality' are left largely with the role of policing those who are defined as 'abnormal', the excluded.

Practice Example

In 1993–4, a number of probation areas used the work of Robert Ross in group-based 'challenges' to offending. The basis of Ross's approach is that a 'considerable number' of offenders have 'development delays in the acquisition of cognitive skills . . . essential for social competence' (Ross, 1990, p. 3).

In Ross's view, many offenders have learning deficits. This model confirms the 'deficit' model of learning difficulty by adding 'criminality' to its list of negatives, and by defining necessary skills for 'social competence' as those which exclude the 'incompetent'. Ross's approach also denies reality. Courts only deal with a very small percentage of offenders (Mayhew and May, 1993; Kelly, 1988; Home Office, 1992). Yet probation officers oppress the offenders they work with by holding them 'responsible' for all offending.

Black 'clients' particularly are placed in the position of representing all black people, in a direct denial of their individuality. They are also more likely to be defined as having learning difficulties (Coard, 1971).

The relevance of anti-racist practice with white 'clients' for black 'clients'

Probation workers are charged with taking on board Section 95 of the Criminal Justice Act 1991, which requires the monitoring of racism. Its implementation is supported by Probation Service area policies and the National Association of Probation Officers. Its use in the office in relation to white 'clients' boils down to responding to 'racist comments'. How frequently this happens has been difficult to monitor. Also, the evidence to date suggests that contact between white workers and white 'clients' is unlikely to raise 'racism' automatically as an issue for consideration.

Practice Example

In one field team with an exclusively white caseload in a predominantly white area, community workers reported very few racist comments being made, therefore the subject was not discussed in team meetings. Yet this location was unpopular with black staff. Black visitors to the town felt high levels of hostility. The term of abuse for the police was 'black bastards'.

Knowing that racism exists but not raising the subject unless in response to a direct comment or action fosters collusion between white workers and 'clients'. White 'clients' who have not had their racism addressed in an outpost office will reveal their racism, thereby affecting black 'clients' and staff, when they come into contact with them in offices in larger conurbations. In describing Probation Service areas south of London, David Reardon of the

Association of Black Probation Officers was very critical of services equating their anti-racist practice and policy with having a black population. As he put it, statements claiming that:

'We don't have many black people in this area, therefore we don't need to adopt anti-racist policies', ignore the fact that Highpoint, Blundeston, Dover, and Maidstone prisons are full up with London based black people. (Reardon, 1993, p. 16)

Probation officers in field offices need to address the issue of racism in the criminal justice system, including prisons, if their anti-racist social work is to be more than tokenistic. Moreover, white 'clients' using probation hostels, on community service, attending probation centres, motor projects and drop-in provisions, joining groups or entering prison may contribute to the racism experienced by black 'clients'. Black 'clients' either put up with the racism, react to the provocation or, where possible, leave the provision. All of these options are at a cost to the black 'client'.

If anti-racism is not brought to a white 'client's' notice during the first contact with the Probation Service, a precedent legitimising its continued absence from other resources will have been established. If an anti-racist response is only made at the point of contact between a white 'client' and either a black 'client' or black worker, white probation officers are failing black people. Not addressing this issue earlier also makes it easier for the white 'client' to isolate the person making an anti-racist response and draw on racist stereotypes to substantiate his or her position. These stereotypes include defining black 'clients' and workers as having 'no sense of humour' or a 'chip on their shoulder', and white workers as 'politically correct'.

Probation officers should find ways of letting black and white 'clients' know about an agency's anti-racist position at the start of their work with them, and inform them about the ways in which the Probation Service will respond to racist behaviour. White workers who only address racism as an issue when a racist incident occurs continue defining racism as black people's problem. Moreover, such responses are reactive rather than preventative, and perpetuate the view that racism is the individual act of a 'bad' white person, thereby ignoring cultural and institutional racism.

Practice Example

One probation hostel staffed by white people accommodated very few black 'clients'. Moreover, those who came stayed a very short time. Meanwhile, a hostel located nearby but run by a black organisation frequently had a waiting list. Some workers held the view that black 'clients' were remanded in custody because black 'clients' were reluctant to use 'white' hostels.

This Practice Example reveals how racism is dumped on black voluntary organisations by statutory services. Black voluntary organisations are often put in the position of filling the gaps left by relatively well-resourced mainstream services. It also exemplifies how easy it is for white workers to miss institutional racism and 'blame the victim', instead of carrying out a careful scrutiny into their own work.

The relevance of anti-racist practice with white 'clients' for black workers

If anti-racist practice is understood only as service delivery to black people, large areas of the country will ignore its relevance to local practice. All areas contain employment, career development and promotion opportunities for all grades of staff. When current or prospective black workers are considering where they want to work, the anti-racist approach of agencies and teams is a significant factor they consider. If teams have not seriously thought about the relevance of anti-racist practice in predominantly white communities, black workers are unlikely to feel welcome in their midst.

The risks black workers face when working in predominantly white agencies in predominantly white communities are compounded when a team maintains that racism is 'not a problem' for them. Good employment practice as well as anti-racist social work demands that all social services and probation teams which serve predominantly white communities raise the question: 'What effect does ignoring racism have on the employment, promotion and retention of black workers?' White workers who feel unable to answer this query should be able to draw on training opportunities which will facilitate their working on raising their consciousness about the issue.

Practice Example

A probation district was unpopular with black workers. This fact was well known to the management of the agency. Indeed, when a black worker positively opted to go to the district, it caused considerable surprise. When recruiting black workers to the service, management gave them posts in other districts. No attempt was made to change policy and practice in the problematic district. This response has two negative outcomes.

First, it fails black workers by creating a 'no go' area, although there is nothing particularly remarkable about this district, similar situations exist elsewhere. The practice of not dealing with the issue is widespread, further restricting employment opportunities for black workers. Moreover, given that Probation Services are introducing mobility policies which give managers the power to direct workers to new posts, black workers could be directed to unsupportive locations when Probation Services feel it contingent to do so.

> *The other negative outcome affects white workers. Most workers were aware of the poor image their district had gained, and wanted changes. Teams made strenuous efforts to alter the district's reputation but received little support in doing so from management. Without managerial endorsement of their attempts, it proved impossible to make effective headway in addressing the problem.*

Management support is crucial in realising organisational change. Managers also need training to become skilled negotiators for the realisation of anti-racist social work.

The relevance of anti-racist practice for white workers

Racism also impacts deleteriously on the quality and integrity of white people's lives. White people *know* about the pervasive nature of racism in this country, but their failure to act on this knowledge makes it difficult for black people to trust white people. The turning of racism into a public issue has enabled white people to recognise racism and how it 'barbs' into them. If such responses are ignored, racism doesn't go away: the white individuals concerned only feel worse.

Racism reduces the opportunities white people have for developing friendships and professional relationships with black people. It reduces the scope that white people have to share, enjoy and learn from the ethnic diversity of the UK. Racism also distorts the quality of white people's lives by perpetuating the unquestioned assumption that white people are superior. The 'casual', sometimes vicious expressions of racism by white people on the bus, in the pub, at sporting events, undermines us all. Failure to become involved in anti-racist practice hurts white workers because public awareness of the issue has altered the ways in which things are seen and heard. Finally, doing nothing about racism causes white people to lose their self-respect.

Practice Example

> *A white probation officer took his nephew and friend to a football match. Both teams had black players. Every time a black player of either team touched the ball, one white man shouted unrestrained racist abuse. Many in the crowd looked at this man and at each other, but nobody said anything. The probation officer said nothing because he was frightened, but he felt the shame of doing so. Racism effects the quality of white people's lives because, instead of enjoying difference, they rely on the myth of superiority to support their fragile egos.*

White people need to overcome their sense of powerlessness and guilt in such situations by taking action against racism. It doesn't have to be either an aggressive or individual act, but some way of distancing themselves and demonstrating their disapproval. Without such action, a black person's experience of a white person who stands against racism but takes no action against racist abuse will be the same as that of the actively racist abuser. Furthermore, it will be marked by disappointment and lack of solidarity in a common struggle.

Conclusions

In this chapter we have highlighted the importance of anti-racist social work training throughout one's working career at the pre-qualifying, qualifying and post-qualifying levels. We have also revealed how the limited progress in the realisation of anti-racist practice has been exaggerated by those who oppose anti-racist social work. We have pinpointed how much work remains to be done for anti-racist social work to permeate the organisational culture of the Probation Service and have an impact on individual workers, 'clients' and teams. Moreover, we have argued the importance of training – whether in college or in-house – in raising both black and white practitioners' consciousness of the issues and equipping them with the practical skills and knowledge for improving practice with both black and white 'clients'.

Senior managers should take responsibility for structuring training opportunities so that those which become available can be tailored more suitably to meeting the specific needs of individual workers and their teams. In this, the importance of white workers working on racism as a matter which deeply implicates them must not be ignored. Nor must the question of improving service delivery to black 'clients' and all other 'clients' be dropped.

5 Challenging racism in prison and throughcare

Black people are over-represented among prisoners in this country, and under-represented among prison staff. As noted in Chapter 1, imprisonment is the final step in a process whereby black people are treated differently from white people at almost every stage of the criminal justice system. The evidence is ambiguous in some areas, and not enough work has been done to explain some of the disparities between the treatment of black and white defendants (Gordon, 1988), but the overall picture is quite clear.

The outcome of institutional and individual racism is that some prisons have more black inmates than white, and almost all hold a disproportionate number of black people (Shallice and Gordon, 1990; HMCIP, 1990; Denney, 1992; Hudson, 1993; HORSD, 1994). Afro-Caribbeans bear the main brunt of this disparity, as the level of imprisonment of Asians is similar to that of whites (Smith, 1994). Overall, by 1994, 16.2 per cent of male and 25.8 per cent of female prisoners in England and Wales were black (HORSD, 1994). So were 19 per cent of adult remand prisoners in 1990 (Dholakia, 1994). Home Office statisticians and some academics have argued that overseas prisoners distort the figures and should, therefore, be excluded (Maden et al., 1992). Even when this is done, the statistics remain disturbing: 12 per cent of male and 14 per cent of female prisoners of British origin are black.

This chapter considers this state of affairs and examines some of the survival strategies open to black prisoners by examining relationships between 'clients' and workers, workers and workers, and employees and their employers. It highlights examples of good practice by black and white probation officers, and constructive Probation Service policies which support it. Research carried out for this chapter into racism from the perspective of prison-based probation officers is referred to where appropriate. This involved a questionnaire completed by probation officers in twelve prisons and a small number of follow-up interviews.

'Clients' and workers

Literature is now readily available which documents the extensive effects of institutional racism on the disproportionate number of black people on remand and sentenced to prison, the relatively small number of black people sentenced to community penalties (see McDermott, 1990; NACRO, 1991; Denney, 1992) and the criminalisation of black people in the UK (Hudson, 1993). Other research, ranging from official reports to personal accounts, gives details of the pervasive personal racism endured by British prisoners. For example, the official inspection of Leeds Prison in 1990 led to an observation by inspectors that prison officers often racially abused black prisoners, and that no provision was made for halal or kosher food. The Home Secretary's response to the report made no comment on such racial abuse and was equivocal about when suitable food would be available to Muslim and Jewish prisoners (Fielding and Fowles, 1991).

Trevor Hercules (1989), in one of the few accounts of the experiences of black prisoners in the UK, wrote that the experience of racism at the hands of uniformed staff varied from one prison to another only in degree. He was prepared to campaign for his and other prisoners' rights, but he makes it clear that this was a risky and costly stance to take:

> Trying to stick up for your right to be a Moslem and eat a Moslem diet, but at the same time knowing you were one of a few men trying alone to confront the system was dispiriting – the consequences could mean not only loss of remission but real physical harm when the swarm of blue uniforms moved in. (Hercules, 1989, pp. 73–4)

He describes the tension between refusing to bow down to racist tyranny on the one hand and the need to avoid falling into bitterness and perpetual struggle on the other.

Genders and Player (1989) found that prisoners were cautious in their complaints about racism, confining them to specific areas of concern. McDermott's (1990) study similarly identified particular causes of complaint rather than a generalised discontent about racism. Both investigations confirmed that failure to provide for special diets remained a contentious issue.

Our research found that prisoners still find it difficult to get the diets required for religious reasons, and that insisting on such provision leads to black inmates being labelled 'troublemakers'. Twenty per cent of the Asian prisoners interviewed in a larger study conducted at about the same time complained about problems in practising their religion, of whom 80 per cent attributed these difficulties to racial discrimination. The same researchers found that a third of Asians and 16 per cent of Afro-Caribbeans experienced discrimination where diet was concerned, with some Muslims and Sikhs getting suitable food only occasionally, if at all. Many Muslims are forced to adopt vegetarian diets because halal meat is not made available (Burnett and Farrell, 1994). Black and anti-racist probation officers we interviewed felt the need to deal with many allegations of racist treatment of inmates informally. They claimed that to take them all to Liaison Committee meetings would reduce officers' effectiveness and bog them down in such committee work.

Complaints about specific incidents are not always satisfactorily resolved, partly because the effectiveness of the formal Race Relations Liaison Committees (RRLOs) varies considerably from one prison to another. Most Race Relations Liaison Officers feel that they have insufficient time to do the job properly, and wing staff prefer to deal with issues informally on an individual basis, which reduces the awareness of the RRLOs and their committees of the scale of the problem (Burnett and Farrell, 1994).

In some prisons the same complaints (for example, concerning special diets) have been taken to the Race Relations Liaison Committee repeatedly without any effect. Indeed, even prisoners who are subjected to racial attacks are reticent about complaining: they too feel that they will be seen as troublemakers, and they are not confident that their complaints will be taken seriously, according to Burnett and Farrell's research. These two authors' study also revealed that less than a quarter of black and white prisoners knew of the existence of Race Relations Liaison Officers (Burnett and Farrell, 1994).

Another contentious area is the discriminatory allocation of less desirable work to black prisoners. Until recently, this concern was also mentioned with monotonous regularity in reports on individual prisons by the Prison Inspectorate. McDermott (1990) noted that, where officers had discretion about which prisoners and cells to search, black prisoners were targeted disproportionately often, and that disciplinary charges for disrespect or disobedience were predominantly against black inmates in the prisons she studied. The Chief Inspector of Prisons, reporting on an inspection of Leicester Prison, quoted a belief by staff that:

> ethnic minority over-representation in disciplinary matters was the consequence of professional inexperience on the part of staff members and, to a lesser extent, of covert racialism. (quoted in NACRO, 1993, p. 12)

Black prisoners (with the exception of Asians) were seven times as likely to complain of racial injustice where disciplinary matters were concerned, according to a recent study (Burnett and Farrell, 1994, p. 21).

Thorough monitoring to eliminate these kinds of discrimination is needed. Although the Prison Department now requires that this be done, the system for doing so has only recently been put into place, and it is too soon to pass judgement on its effectiveness. No action appears to have been taken on earlier monitoring exercises at single prisons, apart from attempts by Race

Relations Liaison Officers to influence future allocation of prisoners to different work sites (see Genders and Player, 1989). Although Burnett and Farrell (1994) have now provided a framework for future research to be systematically carried out in individual establishments in their Prison Department-commissioned publication, it is too early to judge whether it will be used effectively in formal investigations.

Meanwhile, concern about failure of the Prison Service to deal adequately with racism in its establishments continues to mount. Thus the Criminal Justice Consultative Council called for more effective monitoring and greater involvement of black organisations in one of its first reports (Shaw, 1994). McDermott's (1990) research, however, indicates that discretion will be abused, although there are circumstances in which it would be undesirable to reduce uniformed staff's discretion. Staff need encouragement to change their negative attitudes about black people. The provision of good role models by other staff and training can help in this regard. None the less, disciplinary measures are also required in some situations.

The Prison Service *Race Relations Manual* asserts that avoiding racial discrimination is a matter of basic professionalism for uniformed staff. The definition of 'professionalism' it gives is behaving 'in a way which does not allow personal views to affect our behaviour towards other people' (HMPS, 1991a, pp. 1–2). This definition is limited and needs expanding to include an awareness that anti-racist practice is good practice. This understanding, now widespread within the Probation Service, ought to be transferable to the prison setting (see Kett et al., 1992; WYPS, 1993).

A crucial justification for probation throughcare is that it helps to prevent prisoners from becoming isolated and alienated from their homes and communities (Raban, 1987). In the light of evidence about the position of black prisoners, a case can be made for concentrating probation officers' throughcare efforts on black 'clients'. In a context of limited resources following the imposition of cash limits on the Probation Service and the increase in the prison population – again as a result of the 'punitive bifurcation' strategy of the Criminal Justice Acts 1991 and 1993 – prioritising the needs of black prisoners is desirable if the burden of alienation and injustice is to be addressed. The current trend for probation officers to spend less time than in the past working with prisoners' families results in their failure to engage with prisoners by gaining their trust through practical support in some of their practical problems – for example, debt and housing. Moreover, the policy imperative of prioritising 'tackling offending' actually undermines such constructive engagement (Peelo et al., 1991, p. 318).

Prisoners, particularly those serving longer sentences, tend gradually to sever outside links and rely increasingly on inner personal resources rather than community ones. Some disengage entirely for long periods and try not to think about life outside (Zamble and Porporino, 1988; Hercules, 1989;

Williams, 1991). This being so, it seems likely that black prisoners, particularly those serving longer sentences, subjected to constant racism from other inmates and from staff, are likely to feel particularly isolated (Kett et al., 1992, p. 52).

As a member of a Board of Visitors has written, commenting on press allegations of a cover-up after a 'race riot' at the privatised Wolds Remand Prison:

> Prisoners who persistently suffer humiliation, racism and abrogation of human rights do not have freedom to express their frustration as do the public at large. (Jeevanjee, 1993, p. 42)

Black perspectives go largely unheard in prisons, and Jeevanjee is unusual and highly visible as a black member of a Board of Visitors. The few black Board members experience racism from prison staff and receive little support from Boards in challenging this (Worrall, 1994).

Some idea of the kinds of frustration involved for black prisoners trying to challenge racism can be gained from Trevor Hercules's brief account of the events leading up to disturbances while he was at Gartree (1989, Chapter 8). All prisoners experience frustrations and feelings of unfairness, but black prisoners are subject to these in respect of multiple aspects of imprisonment simultaneously – job allocation, searches, food, complaints, disciplinary matters and racial abuse being the most common (see Burnett and Farrell, 1994).

Probation areas have begun to take initiatives aimed at combating the problem of black prisoners' alienation from their communities. In Sheffield, for example, outreach workers make and maintain contact with all newly-remanded black defendants to assist with bail applications and offer traditional befriending. They also run black prisoners' groups in more than one institution, and similar groups are now organised in a number of areas. Through black outreach workers or volunteers, the service aims to provide appropriate support to black prisoners and raise professional awareness of issues specific to their situation (although most Probation Services' published policy documents have little to say about professional practice initiatives of this kind).

Prison-based probation staff also need to pay particular attention to the needs and demands of black inmates. This is especially important at the very beginning of their remand or induction period, in order to provide information, assess needs and ensure that relevant services are available (NAPO, 1991; Kett et al., 1992). This suggests that field probation staff should pay particularly close attention to liaising effectively with clients' prison probation officers at these times – which is good practice in any event.

Some probation officers have shown signs of undue reticence about their ability to work effectively with black clients. Counter-productive, guilt-inducing types of 'race awareness training' (Sivanandan, 1985; Tonkin, 1987) have led some officers to avoid contact with black clients for fear of giving offence. The outcome has been an unintended discrimination (Denney, 1992; Voakes and Fowler, 1989; Alibhai, 1988) which has had extremely serious consequences. With court reports failing to make persuasive arguments for community supervision, even more black defendants are going to prison as a result.

There are clear implications for probation work, both in the community and in custodial institutions. For one thing, these research findings should encourage probation officers to see racism more realistically. Racism is not confined to the boorish and the bigoted. Its subtle forms need constant monitoring throughout the system, and action must be taken whenever they are detected. The fact that we have made mistakes in the past should not paralyse us in taking action now. Understanding the mechanisms involved gives us insights into how racism can be tackled. In the present context, monitoring reports presented to courts and different decision-making bodies within prisons (for example, with reference to allocation to particular types of prison after sentencing, early release, home leave, allocation of security category) go some way in achieving this.

Probation officers' contact with different categories of 'clients' should also be monitored at all stages of their work. If they are inadvertently discrimi-nating against 'clients' at the Pre-Sentence Report stage, they are likely to continue doing so when making decisions about throughcare. Challenging, angry 'clients' make particular demands upon probation officers: they tend to be seen as 'difficult to work with'. The classic response of maintaining minimal levels of contact with 'troublesome clients' is inappropriate. Given that black 'clients' wish to minimise their encounters with such damaging interventions, it is not surprising to find – albeit anecdotal – evidence that black prisoners are less likely than white people to take up voluntary after-care (Celnick, 1993; NACRO, 1991). To engage effectively with black prisoners, white probation officers in particular need to make additional efforts, and senior staff must insist upon this principle.

Monitoring the frequency of contact with black 'clients' compared to that with whites (as suggested in Kett et al., 1992; NAPO, 1991), however, will not be enough. More subtle measures of the quality of service provided will be required if we are to avoid a situation where black 'clients' receive a second-class service and expect less. Probation officers will have to get into the habit of explicit negotiation about black prisoners' needs and expectations (Williams, 1992). Ascertaining needs through discussion with 'clients' is a matter of good practice with all 'clients'.

The problems of alienation may be less intense for black inmates in prisons with a substantial black population. On the other hand, black prisoners are more likely to be perceived as a problem by prison management when the number of black inmates becomes significant. At that point, groups of black prisoners are 'shipped out' of some prisons to keep the numbers down (Genders and Player, 1989). This practice needs to be rigorously opposed by probation teams as well as by governors. The consequences of frequent and unnecessary moves for individuals are serious. They disrupt family contacts and effective throughcare work, and the underlying racism revealed by such policies must be challenged and brought to the attention of local Race Relations Liaison Committees and, if necessary, reported to the Commission for Racial Equality and the Criminal Justice Consultative Council. Moving members of particular, identifiable groups of prisoners to prevent concentration in one prison arises from a belief that black people represent a problem by their sheer presence. This kind of attitude is quite unacceptable.

White prison officers fear that black prisoners are potentially troublesome because they will combine to resist illegitimate use of authority. They focus on Afro-Caribbean men because they consider this group of inmates most anti-authority. They seek to prevent the concentration of black inmates in particular parts of prisons, in the belief that 'inter-racial power struggles would inevitably break out unless the proportion of Black prisoners is controlled' (Genders and Players, 1989, p. 133). As these authors point out, this kind of thinking derives from a prejudice which sees black people as an 'invading force', swamping the 'rightful occupants' by sheer numbers. The imposition of anti-racist policies offers an opportunity for explicit challenges to such racist presuppositions.

Most of the larger Probation Services now advise their staff to use interpreters where appropriate when working with prisoners whose first language is not English. The prison setting is an important one in this respect. Remand prisoners need culturally-sensitive advice in their own language to help them make rational decisions about bail applications and the conduct of their trials. The Inner London Probation Service has pioneered an information pack for foreign prisoners and a court guide in a number of languages in addition to English (ILPS, 1993). The Kent Probation Service has a similar pack. The existence of policies and clear procedures on the use of interpreters is a prerequisite for good professional practice. Unfortunately, the extent to which these policies are applied in practice, leaves room for improvement (Casale, 1989; Baker et al., 1991). Some services have acknowledged that the provision of interpreters needs further attention (for example, MAPS, 1991). Interpretation facilities are not always easy for officers to arrange. Moreover, in some areas, interpreters have had only rudimentary training for working with probation 'clients'.

Group work with black prisoners is becoming more common, allowing issues of concern to black 'clients' to be addressed appropriately and encouraging the development of specialisms by field staff (Towl, 1993). Such groups now exist in prisons whose inmates come from major centres of black population, including those organised by probation staff from Huddersfield,

Luton, Nottingham and Sheffield (NACRO, 1991; SYPS, undated).

Some of the larger, urban Probation Services have also initiated projects beginning at the pre-sentence stage to ensure that overseas prisoners are treated equitably. This is particularly important where defendants arrive at major ports and airports (Abernethy and Hammond, 1992; ILPS, 1993). Until recently, no Pre-Sentence Reports were prepared for foreign defendants' court appearances, and any children accompanying them were vulnerable to care proceedings. Provision of improved information to courts is a first step to challenging such injustices. Such work has been pioneered by the London, Kent and Sussex probation areas.

Group work with black prisoners whose first language is not English is not easy. Specific provision for foreign prisoners may be necessary. Such work is currently at a very early stage. The Probation Service's record to date, where foreign offenders are concerned, is unimpressive (Cheney, 1993, 1994; Tarzi and Hedges, 1990). Legal changes mean that this will have to improve. Apart from anything else, the right to consideration for conditional release involves probation officers in routine work with prisoners from abroad in quite a new way.

Despite evidence that the Race Relations Liaison Officer system is not meeting foreign prisoners' needs, the prison service has declined to take any new initiative. The Prison Reform Trust has argued that a separate section is needed at prison service headquarters to deal with issues relating to prisoners from abroad because their needs are marginalised by treating them as a 'race relations issue'. However, no changes were made in response (Shaw, 1993, p. 10).

The Probation Service, for its part, is beginning to acknowledge the need for awareness of immigration and deportation issues and willingness to campaign on them. These are intensely political matters, and involvement by official agencies is bound to be controversial if the view of the dominant political group is questioned. Nevertheless, serious engagement with black communities is bound to raise the issue of the UK's and the European Union's immigration policies and their impact upon black people – including those born in the UK.

The best way forward in the short term will be for Probation Services to use their powers to fund partnerships with voluntary sector organisations with expertise in this area. Many probation 'clients' come into contact with the immigration authorities as a result of routine processing by the police. It is not, therefore, just a matter of detecting individuals who have overstayed their visa limits or violated other immigration rules. The police make immigration enquiries about many black people whose nationality is not in question. The Probation Service may be in a position to take this matter up, along with the voluntary groups working in the area. The political sensitivity arises because most of the groups with which services might consider entering into partnerships are not only advice agencies, they also use the information and expertise gained through individual casework for campaigning purposes (CADP, 1992).

Interactions between staff

There are few black staff in UK prisons. Only 5 per cent of probation officers in the UK are black. Considerably fewer are likely to be working in prisons, but there are no published statistics available to verify this. The numbers are likely to be lowered by the unattractiveness of prison-based employment, given serving probation officers' reluctance to volunteer for secondment to prisons.

Even fewer black staff work as prison officers, and recruitment is unlikely to alter this balance in the near future as less than 3 per cent of new recruits to the prison service in 1992 were black, and that was the highest figure ever (Butler, 1993; Ward, 1994). Given that these recruits were added to an almost insignificant number of existing black workers, the level of recruitment would have to rise dramatically in order for the proportion of black staff to approach a representative level. However, progress in this respect has been made recently. In 1992, there were only 70 black prison officers out of a total of 23,000 – less than 0.3 per cent (NACRO, 1992a). By 1994 this had risen to 2.1 per cent (Grimwood, 1994). These were distributed as follows: 0.5 per cent at governor grade and 2.2 per cent at officer grades (Grimwood, 1994). In addition, 41 per cent of prison medical officers and 10.6 per cent of nursing grades are black (Grimwood, 1994). Black uniformed officers, though, are likely to suffer added disadvantage because they are in such a small minority and lack the support of a significant number of black colleagues.

Like women staff, black prison officers are placed under considerable pressure to ignore offensive behaviour and comments with good grace. Their full membership of the workplace group depends on being seen as a 'good sport' (Ellis, 1993). Five of the 12 black prison officers interviewed by Burnett and Farrell (1994) had been racially victimised by other members of staff in the preceding three months. White probation staff sometimes collude with such expectations, adding to black officers' difficulties (see NAPOWYPSB, 1987). In our research, probation officers discounted their observations of discriminatory behaviour towards black staff by describing racist language as being 'intended as good-natured banter'.

Such situations pose a difficult dilemma for black workers: should they go along with their own humiliation in order to get the job done? In an occupation where there is at times some physical threat from prisoners, the need for acceptance by colleagues is greater than in other types of work.

The response of black officers is further complicated by white staff associating black people in general with disorder. As Gilroy (1987, p. 109) points out: 'The association of criminality and disorder with black people is a central feature of racist ideology.' Such images underpin 'the attitudes of many of the actors on the criminal justice stage' (Alfred, 1992, p. 8). Moreover, such stereotypes are not located solely within the ranks of the prison inmates, for:

> Prison officers tended to empathise with the feelings they projected onto the White prisoners, perceiving Blacks as an invading force. (Genders and Player, 1989, p. 133)

Given the polarised 'us and them' relations between uniformed staff and inmates in most prisons, it is hardly surprising that black prison officers – regarded by many white officers as members of a troublesome group – are up to twice as likely to identify colleagues rather than inmates as the group that causes them most stress at work (Alfred, 1992; Jacobs and Grear, 1977). Black staff often find that their authority is undermined by white colleagues' attitudes, thereby increasing stress levels, particularly if inmates' racist language goes unchallenged by white officers.

This is highly likely to happen when so many white staff find racist language and jokes acceptable. As one black prison officer has been quoted as saying:

> I feel so isolated. The blacks think I'm part of the establishment and the whites think I have a chip on my shoulder because I won't laugh at ethnic jokes. (McDermott, 1990, p. 223)

According to the Criminal Justice Consultative Council's report, *Race and the Criminal Justice System*, the problem of isolation is susceptible to improvement by those deciding upon prison officers' postings (see Shaw, 1994). Yet black prison officers are often sent to work in prisons with hardly any other black staff, and this seems to serve no particular operational purpose.

Another black officer told McDermott:

> I walk into the mess and conversation stops. And yet I'm sitting in the wing office and one of my fellow officers starts complaining about black neighbours moving in and bringing down house prices. And I'm sitting right there! (1990, p. 223)

As McDermott notes, this officer is both too visible by virtue of his colour, and invisible when it suits his colleagues to pretend that 'race' is not an issue. For him, it is always going to be an issue while he has to put up with this kind of behaviour.

In a misguided attempt to warn would-be black staff of the likely pressures from inmates, selection interviewers have taken to asking black – but not white – candidates for posts in the Prison Service hypothetical questions about how they would handle racist comments or over-familiar approaches from black inmates.

> The message from such differentiated interviewing is that black officers need to be able to deal with racism, rather than one which undertakes to eliminate racism so that black officers no longer need to deal with it. The latter approach would involve anti-racist interviewers in asking questions which are designed to elicit whether a candidate holds racist attitudes, or is committed to the race relations policy. (Alfred, 1992, p. 28; see also Alibhai-Brown, 1988)

We would add that such encounters also indicate how anti-racist work is erroneously treated as a matter that makes no direct demands on white officers.

The scarcity of black prison officers tends to reinforce racist stereotyping and their treatment as 'a remarkably homogeneous group' (OPCS, 1985, p. 22). It also legitimises the failure of white prison officers to challenge their colleagues' racist attitudes and beliefs (Genders and Player, 1989). The failure to recruit black staff to senior positions also casts doubt on the Prison Department's commitment to its equal opportunities policy where staffing is concerned.

This state of affairs persists despite the guidance made available to staff in 1991. This made it clear that racist jokes and 'derogatory terms even when used in a light-hearted context, are offensive', and that prison officers should 'challenge racially abusive language wherever they encounter it ... from prisoners or other staff' (HMPS, 1991, pp. 85–6). Earlier guidance on 'race' issues has been resented by many staff (Genders and Player, 1989), and only a quarter of prison officers surveyed in 1994 had read the *Race Relations Manual* (Burnett and Farrell, 1994). But the manual now implies that using racist language is a disciplinary offence. The number of cases considered under its rubric is unknown, but according to the Prison Service's Director of Personnel and Finance, there have been some. In addition, these rules will be strengthened if the trade unions are successful in gaining acceptance of a new code of discipline containing racial harassment as a specific offence (Butler, 1993). The promise to recruit staff throughout the Prison Service 'entirely on merit' and ethnically monitor the results should also improve matters (HMPS, 1991, p. 98). The manual also draws attention to, but does not advocate, the legal possibility of positive action to improve the recruitment of under-represented groups (HMPS, 1991, p. 100). This move could also be beneficial.

Probation officers are marginalised in the power structure of prisons. Prison secondments are unpopular with field probation staff in most areas, and their union has campaigned for some years to withdraw prison-based probation officers to free them to offer a service from outside (Williams,

1991, 1992). Now that prison governors are in a position to buy in welfare services – not necessarily from the statutory Probation Service – this debate has become increasingly irrelevant, but it has done little to strengthen the influence of probation officers in prisons. Nevertheless, NAPO has continued to advocate withdrawal as part of an anti-racist strategy (NAPO, 1991), despite attempts to overturn the policy (Schofield, 1994).

Prison probation officers should take a more pro-active role on 'race' issues. Local areas' throughcare and anti-racism or equal opportunities policies have begun to advocate supporting the work of Race Relations Liaison Officers and making a constructive contribution to Race Relations Management Teams (see, for example, SYPS, 1993). This initiative is also encouraged in the *Race Relations Manual* (HMPS, 1991, p. 121) and by NAPO (NAPO, 1991). Although Race Relations Liaison Officers need more support (Genders and Player, 1989, p. 149), change in this area can be successfully brought about:

> Changes are feared, but opposition is largely dissipated once they have been incorporated into the daily routine of prison life. This must provide at least some modest grounds for optimism. (Genders and Player, 1989, p. 47)

All black staff working in prisons need support structures, and these are presently inadequate in some areas, where a single black officer is in a very isolated position.

Involvement in the official structure for dealing with racist incidents is a strategy pursued by the majority of probation staff who responded to our research questionnaire. Usually, one team member (often the senior officer) represents the probation staff on the prison's Race Relations Management Team or its equivalent. The consequences of doing so were mixed. Some respondents noted that the RRLO Committee was inactive or mainly a 'paper exercise', and others said that their representative pursued a 'softly, softly' strategy to avoid alienating staff from other disciplines. Such approaches may succeed in achieving some change, but they also run the risk of colluding with racism to protect good working relationships.

Other strategies described by respondents included highlighting the prison's equal opportunities policy during induction programmes for new prisoners, taking individual complaints up with senior staff, and supporting and guiding inmates with grievances through the appropriate procedures.

In the short term, prison probation teams could do more to improve matters for black prisoners and staff by concentrating some effort on assisting or pressuring RRLOs to implement stated Prison Department policy. McDermott (1990, p. 225) observed that the RRLOs she interviewed often did the job in the face of 'ridicule and resentment from their fellow officers' and with insufficient support from senior staff. In the longer term, more commitment will be needed from the Prison Service to ensure that RRLOs have enough time, influence and funding to do the job properly. Until this is forthcoming, a degree of cynicism about the commitment to change will remain justified.

The ambiguous role probation officers in prisons hold leads to their being given enormous amounts of work which is of questionable benefit to their 'clients', but useful to the maintenance of the prison ethos and regime (Priestley, 1972). Without abandoning the much-maligned 'welfare' work which provides the opportunity to make the first contact with many 'clients' (Williams, 1991), seconded staff teams can usefully review the regime-maintenance activities and discard some of them (or give them lower priority) as part of an anti-racist strategy. Pursuing such an option will not be easy in an era of contractual relationships between governors and chief probation officers. Although progress in clarifying the probation role in prisons may be slow, this accords with the equal opportunities policies advocated by the Prison Department, the Home Office and the Probation Service. Initiatives aimed at clarifying the role of prison probation officers are also endorsed in NAPO's (1991, p. 12) anti-racist strategy.

In short, probation officers in prisons need to concentrate their efforts if their anti-racist policies are to have any impact on prison bureaucracies which are very resistant to change. As Kett et al. put it:

> It will clearly be more productive more quickly to look first to those areas over which the Service has complete control or full responsibility before moving on to more difficult arenas where its input is either not welcome or not influential. (1992, p. 52)

Hence, devising anti-racist team strategies will be particularly challenging for probation officers in prisons. They will need to review and clarify their priorities and challenge some of the expectations of other staff. If additional support is to be given to black prisoners and their families, care will need to be taken to ensure that this does not lead to black 'clients' being targeted for extra surveillance: good practice is negotiated, not imposed.

Such good practice by probation officers – particularly where 'race' and gender issues are concerned – often leads to conflict with prison officers. This is ignored in the first edition of the *Race Relations Manual*, which does not include probation teams in its list of staff responsibilities. However, this omission has been rectified in some prisons through contracts for the provision of services drawn up between governors and Chief Probation Officers. The manual emphasises that: 'the implementation of the Service's race relations policy is the responsibility of all members of staff' (HMPS, 1991, p. 105). Such provisions legitimise the implementation of team anti-racist policies in prisons, as does Section 95 of the Criminal Justice Act 1991. Probation officers can no longer argue that it is impossible or discourteous to try to implement their anti-racist policies in hostile 'host' institutions. If this argument ever had any validity, it is indefensible in the context of the Probation and Prison Services' current policies (Kett et al., 1992, p. 52).

Given the lack of support offered to black staff in the Prison Service, even when sympathetic white colleagues exist (Alfred, 1992; McDermott, 1990), and in the Probation Service (Divine, 1991; Fletcher, 1988; Mavunga, 1993), it is perhaps hardly surprising that black people are not coming forward in large numbers to work in prisons. Moreover, it is difficult to retain black staff when they do, although there are too many recent recruits for firm conclusions to be drawn about this trend (see Jeevanjee, 1993; Ward, 1994). Black officers do have an important role to play if their working environment can be improved. The black prisoners' groups mentioned above are largely resourced by field staff who do not have to work in the prison full-time. Their contribution to anti-racist struggles is, none the less, vital. Black probation officers who do work in prisons mention 'clients' who would not have engaged with white colleagues, but have with them, which indicates a particular unmet need. White staff confirm that there are individuals and situations best dealt with by black colleagues.

Black staff's awareness of racism directed at them by 'clients' can be complicated by the simultaneous awareness of the 'sophisticated' racism of their colleagues, or the less sophisticated use of racist jokes and language, with the associated expectation that black staff 'join in with the joke' (NAPOWYPSB, 1987, p. 9). Most of the white prison-based probation officers responding to the questionnaire about racism in prisons were optimistic. A minority felt that it was not a problem at all. The majority felt that racist comments and behaviour were being challenged appropriately when they arose.

Employees and employers

The Prison Service has a much-praised equal opportunities policy (Faulkner, 1985 quoted in NACRO, 1986; Alibhai, 1988; Home Office, 1991, 1991a), but prisons remain an extremely hostile environment for black staff (Alfred, 1992; Day et al., 1989; Genders and Player, 1989; McDermott, 1990; Mills, 1993). Anti-discriminatory policies are being put into practice, but only up to a point (HMCIP, 1992). The administrative aspects of the policy are proving easier to implement than its wider spirit (Alfred, 1992).

No doubt this 'implementation gap' occurs for some of the reasons applicable to all national policies which have to be applied at local level:

> The experience of the Prison Service is a good example of how very difficult it can be to translate written policies and statements into effective action at every level of a large, dispersed organisation with many long-standing traditions and methods of working. (NACRO, 1992, p. 16)

But where race equality policies are concerned, there is an additional factor: institutional inertia is created by personal reluctance to accept that racism is an abuse of power occurring routinely in one's own workplace. Research indicates that this form of denial occurs in various parts of the criminal justice system (Denney, 1992; Holdaway, 1991, 1991a; Holdaway and Mantle, 1992; Mann, 1993; HMIP, 1993a). Probation officers, police, magistrates, academics and hostel staff all find reasons for not implementing antiracist policies. The rationales for such responses include a lack of confidence in their own ability to work effectively with black 'clients' and denial that racial injustice exists in their area of influence.

Our criminal justice system operates by individualising offending, with sentencers resisting structural analyses of sentencing patterns. By sentencing each 'case' on its merits, overall patterns of discrimination in sentencing are obscured. The commitment to treating each defendant as a unique individual may have a sound and enlightened basis, but it:

> makes it very difficult for sentencer members of [probation] committees to perceive any threads of continuity that link cases of similar or at first sight different types. A case-by-case approach, for example, does not sit easily with one that finds a thread of discrimination running through magistrates' decision-making. (Holdaway and Mantle, 1992, p. 127; see also Hudson, 1993)

This sentencing culture masks discriminatory decision-making, but it does manifest itself in magistrates' decision-making as members of Probation Committees. Although the magistrates will have less influence, this effect is unlikely to change as the committees become smaller, more streamlined Probation Boards. The case-by-case mode of thinking is likely to dominate amongst the magistrate members of such bodies. Chief Probation Officers told Holdaway and Mantle (1992, p. 129) that Probation Committees were often obstacles to change where issues of 'race' policy were concerned, albeit by means of 'inertia rather than a more active form of opposition'.

There is also an ambivalence within the Home Office about introducing and implementing effective anti-racist policies. They form part of a radical agenda implicitly rejected by the government in favour of what one commentator has called 'determined inaction' (Spencer, 1993, p. 30).

Even the limited monitoring of 'improper discrimination' was added to the Criminal Justice Act 1991 as a late amendment, watered down sufficiently to make it impossible for the government to oppose it. When it comes to implementation, the Home Office manages to avoid innovation. The failure to spell out exactly what 'positive action' might mean in practice, for example, is a tactic that has been used repeatedly to block movement over the years (Nixon, 1980, 1984). In the words of Nixon:

> in maintaining a noticeably neutral position on the more innovatory parts of the

policy (primarily on the scope for positive discrimination) and on the more con-troversial action required to implement it (a system of monitoring) the Home Office leaves a lingering impression that it was still waiting for someone to fire the starting pistol. (1984, p. 49)

The outcome of this inertia and conservatism is serious. Black staff are increasingly cynical about the motives of managers who frame high-sound-ing policy and do little to bring it into effect (WMPS, 1986; Gordon, 1988; Prashar, 1987). Added to the crisis of racial injustice in prisons, there is a pro-found legitimisation crisis (Cavadino and Dignan, 1992; Sim, 1994; Sparks, 1994). As the Woolf Report (Woolf, LJ, 1991) noted, people who feel unjustly treated can become volatile. But where racism is concerned, the government seems able to tolerate a high level of discontent, and easily pathologise force-ful responses. Such leadership makes it easier for criminal justice workers to see black people rather than racism as the problem to be addressed. Consequently, much work remains to be done before 'black' will be dissoci-ated from the 'problem' (HMIP, 1993, p. 49).

The experience of black staff

The idea that the workforce of the criminal justice agencies should reflect the racial balance of the wider population has been slow to gain acceptance. In the police force, it was explicitly rejected by the Police Federation as recently as 1980. Only after the publication of the Scarman Report the following year was the under-representation of black people within the police accepted as unjust (Holdaway, 1991). A similar position regarding the need for recruit-ment of black staff was adopted by the probation employers' organisation in 1983, also as a result of Scarman (Denney, 1992; CCPC, 1983). In the Prison Service, the move towards a representative workforce was first touched upon in 1983 in a circular instruction. However, targeted recruitment did not begin until 1990 (Butler, 1993; see also Jeevanjee, 1993).

Each of the agencies has gradually accepted that equal opportunities in recruitment require more than a mere statement of policy. The Prison Service's outreach campaign increased the number of black staff appointed, but only to 59 (2.4 per cent of recruits) in 1991–2 and 180 in the first 41 weeks of 1993 (Ward, 1994). Work on recruiting black graduates to the Accelerated Promotion Scheme began in 1993 (Butler, 1993) but it appears to have got off to a very slow start. Although the rate of retention of black staff has been better in prisons than in probation (Ward, 1994), there is some evidence that black recruits do leave on being posted to prisons a long way from home (Ellis, 1993).

If the will to deal with white colleagues' racism and recruit black people to management grades exists, these difficulties can be overcome more readily.

At least in the Prison Service black staff do not have to start from pre-qualification grades to make their way to the higher ranks which hold a greater degree of power, as is the case in the Probation Service.

However, black probation officers seconded to work in prisons remain largely isolated. Support systems are lacking, beyond those available to all prison probation officers, and little is being done at present to remedy this situation.

The employers' position

In the wake of the 1981 and 1985 inner-city 'riots', the Central Council of Probation Committees (now the Central Probation Council) made an attempt to stimulate a debate about the role of the Probation Service. It published a discussion paper (CCPC, 1986) which identified new and wider responsibilities for its members, including speaking out on behalf of the Probation Service's work with under-privileged individuals and communities.

Interestingly, research on policy-making by probation committees noted in 1992 that:

> the response of area probation committees to this paper ... [was] that very few indeed had taken any action on the basis of it. (Holdaway and Mantle, 1992, p. 131)

In view of Holdaway and Mantle's other findings referred to above, this outcome is not surprising. This tentative beginning appears to have faltered in the face of the institutional inertia of Probation Committees and Services across the country.

Similarly, the Association of Chief Probation Officers (ACOP) has made some moves to open up the debate about the handling of 'race' issues within the service. It set up a Race Issues Working Party which circulated a number of papers in 1986 and provided a conference platform for members of the Association of Black Probation Officers to summarise the extent of racial injustice in the administration of the criminal justice system and to call for systematic action. Research was commissioned to monitor progress (Holdaway and Allaker, 1990), and the implementation of its recommendations is in turn being monitored. This activity preceded, and was therefore not in response to, the Home Office policy announced in Circular No. 75/88 (Home Office, 1988), which required local services to devise and publicise comprehensive policy statements on 'race' issues. This laudable statement claimed that:

> The Home Office is wholly committed to the elimination of racial discrimination from all aspects of the work of the Probation Service, and to a policy of racial equality. There must be no racial discrimination of any kind, conscious or inadvertent. (Home Office, 1988, Annex A, para. 1)

The momentum for change it inspired continued for several years, culminating in the passage of Section 95 of the Criminal Justice Act 1991. Under a new Home Secretary and different senior civil servants, the political situation changed dramatically, and the impetus for change was thwarted. Reports arising from the implementation of Section 95 merely reiterated research findings, without any action plan being devised to tackle the inequalities described (Home Office, 1992).

However, the Association of Black Probation Officers ensured that the momentum was not lost. Probation Services were pressed by ABPO and NAPO to carry out plans hastily prepared in response to the Home Office circular, and some innovative projects and practices, some of which have been described earlier, emerged during a period of nearly five years when the political climate was conducive to constructive change. When this ceased to be the case, the challenge faced by services, innovative projects and committed individuals, was to survive in the face of increasingly unashamed hostility towards equal opportunities from central government. The days when a Home Office circular unequivocally opposed racial discrimination began to seem very remote.

We suggested in Chapter 2 that anti-racist probation practice must, if it is to be more than tokenistic, go beyond monitoring compliance with equal opportunities policies. In this chapter, however, we have repeatedly referred to the need for monitoring. This is because, as we pointed out at the beginning of the chapter, the Prison Service has a commendable policy which is not being fully implemented. The policy rhetoric can be used by anti-racist practitioners in a positive way, and drawing attention to the Prison Service's own policies is likely to be more effective than appealing to those of outside Probation Services.

Purposeful throughcare work is more difficult than ever to sustain at present. Probation Services face cash limits which constrain mileage budgets, and prison governors are purchasing in a newly-created internal market. The principles and aims of prison probation departments need to be made increasingly explicit in the face of this situation. A prominent role in taking forward the Prison Service's 'race' relations policy and practice is clearly important for probation officers working with prisoners.

6 Conclusions: Past failures, new hopes

Racism continues to be an issue which the criminal justice system in general and the Probation Service in particular need to address as a matter of urgency. For, despite the various initiatives which have been undertaken to tackle it, black people's encounters with the criminal justice system – whether as workers or 'clients' – do not affirm their strengths and potential.

As workers, people with black perspectives can and do make innovations in practice which aim to ensure that social justice and respect – traditional values in social work for all 'clients' – are the norm. But the fact that they do so can be experienced as threatening by individuals who are concerned with not upsetting either the current order or managers in resource-starved welfare organisations. Indeed, for the former, the mere presence of a black worker is taken as evidence demonstrating that their position has been undermined. Their reactions draw heavily on stereotypes about black workers which are liberally sprinkled with notions of 'dangerousness' and 'pathology'. These provide the ammunition for fuelling a backlash against anti-racist or even equal opportunities initiatives (Morris, 1994).

As 'clients', black people are more likely to be responded to as 'problems' who need to be controlled rather than assisted to take control of their lives. Hence, their experiences of professionals within the criminal justice system remain oppressive. In probation, these workers' efforts can be limited to ensuring that the minimal reporting conditions under National Standards are complied with, rather than engaging in more supportive forms of interaction which recognise the offender as a person who must be responded to with respect and dignity while having his or her access to welfare resources facilitated.

Some readers will be concerned that such responses privilege offenders over non-offenders. Our reply to such charges is that our way of proceeding is consistent with:

- the traditional value base of social work;
- the fact that being on a Probation Order in itself is the punishment;
- the parameters of the work being those of enabling people to gain control over their lives to make a positive contribution to society;
- the fact that perpetuating injustice on one group of marginalised and oppressed people (offenders) as an excuse for not doing something for other marginalised and oppressed groups (non-offenders) is morally and ethically unacceptable.

Dealing systematically with other oppressed and marginalised people to eliminate the injustice done to them is also something that society must undertake. If working with offenders is one way of moving towards that goal, then it can become one way of challenging society to do likewise with others. Such action is morally justifiable. It is also consistent with good practice. Good practice with others is an anticipated outcome of practice carried out from anti-racist and black perspectives.

White probation officers also under-achieve as long as racism persists. Not only do they not live up to their professional value base of treating others with respect and dignity, thereby further pathologising and oppressing black people, but they also fail to acknowledge their own complicity in maintaining racist interactions. This state of affairs is more likely to arise in institutions which do not have anti-racist initiatives embedded in a practice which acknowledges that anti-racist practice involves their working on themselves as well as improving service delivery and working conditions for black people.

Racism is a complex phenomenon which has destructive processes as well as destructive outcomes. The interaction between its personal, institutional and cultural forms limits the effectiveness of simple 'anti-racist' responses which address only one dimension of it. Action on one of these fronts must be endorsed by action along the others if gains are to be sustained in the long term, although it does not have to be the same person doing everything. If we are to avoid past failures in anti-racist struggles, our future actions must take this understanding on board. It can then become the thread that links different individual and organisational initiatives together in one common struggle – the elimination of racism through anti-racist action for the creation of a non-racist world. In this chapter, we will consider what this means in practice by identifying what needs to be done in each of the three themes we have considered in our book: worker–'client' relationships; employee–employee relationships; and employer–employee interaction. In this way we hope to learn from past failures, use their lessons to transcend the difficulties these identify, and move with new hope into the future.

Worker–'client' relationships

Probation officers, court workers and magistrates hold considerable power over 'clients'. The nature of this power must be acknowledged by workers and 'unpacked' with 'clients' if their work together is to reflect the values of social justice and respect (the right to be treated with dignity). The process whereby work is carried out should be enabling, and not punitive. Indeed, probation officers' role as social workers is not to *punish* people as such, but to help them acquire the knowledge, skills and confidence to lead socially useful lives. In this context, control – in the sense of preventing people from harming themselves and others – is appropriate. Control as surveillance for institutional purposes – such as rationing resources in an inequitable manner or keeping people in their predetermined place – does not encourage the development of trusting relationships which can be used to facilitate change and progress in either individuals or institutions. Nor does it provide a context within which advocacy services for the provision of resources which meet black people's needs as black people and white workers' needs as anti-racist workers can be promoted. Hence, it should not be unduly emphasised.

Instead, probation officers should concentrate on working in partnership with 'clients' to address both the *personal role* they play in committing offences and the *social backdrop* against which this behaviour takes place. Besides working on the specifics of the offence, this means:

- recognising that racism in all its forms plays a crucial role in limiting the opportunities that black people have to lead full and rewarding lives;
- considering the impact of racism at every point in

  – the lives of the individual 'clients' that they work with as probation officers;
  – their encounters with colleagues and courts;
  – their interaction with both black and white communities;

- addressing the issue of racism at the societal level by raising it as a political issue and networking with other individuals and organisations working towards the elimination of racism by promoting anti-racist initiatives.

Worker–worker relationships

Workplace relations that promote anti-racist practice are the concern of every employee in the Probation Service as well as the criminal justice system more generally. The conditions under which both black and white probation workers operate have to be conducive to the realisation of this goal.

But equality in the workplace requires the transformation of working relations. Equality of outcomes cannot be achieved by drafting black workers in to take their share of existing workloads and endorse current definitions of the work to be performed. Different priorities in what is done and how it is done will need to prevail. These will have to include:

- more accountability to service users and the communities they stem from;
- the creation of more relevant and innovative services which do not pathologise 'client' groups;
- the involvement of community groups, victim survivors and offenders in the redefinition of probation practice and the policies guiding it;
- the involvement of both black and white probation officers in developing anti-racist probation practice.

Transforming working relations requires white workers to listen carefully to each other and take seriously evaluations of their practice made by black workers and service users. Reacting defensively is a sure means of blocking communications and the opportunities for learning from each other. Recognising differences in experiences across the racial divide, valuing black people's contributions to the work, and using these to establish equality are critical in creating an environment which is open to innovative work aimed at eradicating racist practices and policies.

Paying attention to process – that is, *how* relationships will be transformed – is as important as what they are being changed to. Incorporating process and outcomes into the analysis and practice of social change enables anti-racist practitioners to avoid a mechanistic and deterministic approach to what needs to be changed and how. It will also facilitate the development of critical, reflective practitioners who can address the complexities of the issues facing them with greater confidence. They will *not* be afraid of making mistakes, owning up to them and learning from them. It also allows white workers to use their own understandings to develop anti-racist practice, instead of casting black workers in the role of 'experts' on the subject and dumping the responsibility for progress on anti-racist practice development onto them.

Employer–employee interaction

The responsibility for changing the culture of an organisation, its policies and its practices cannot be left solely in the hands of practitioners. Managers carry responsibility on this count too. Moreover, managers, particularly those at line management levels – for example, senior probation officers – are subjected to pressures from both above and below (Eley, 1989). Caught in a pincer movement between the demands of their political overlords and grassroots disaffection with the lack of input into decision-making processes, they can form alliances with both practitioners and users to effect change more conducive to anti-racist practice. Thus, acting in concert with others can become a source of empowerment for line managers committed to advancing egalitarian working relations and arguing for the resources which make anti-racist services possible. Ultimately, however, the transformation of workplace relations will also require a redefinition of the organisation's management function (Durrant, 1989). The greater involvement of service users and practitioners in policy formulation and service development will necessitate more democratic, accountable and participative forms of management.

Yet the existence of supportive managers can be seen as but a stepping stone in the path of achieving organisational change. Other changes will have to proceed alongside their emergence. These include:

- redefining the norms which are embedded in the organisational culture of the Probation Service and which guide probation policies and practices;
- securing legislative changes which will underpin anti-racist initiatives in the Probation Service and the criminal justice system more generally;
- engaging with other segments of the criminal justice system – for example, the police, the judiciary, the Prison Service – to obtain changes which will promote anti-racist practice in these quarters as well;
- arguing for the resources which are necessary to develop both staff and service provisions in anti-racist directions;
- turning training into an important element of planned staff development and in promoting the development of anti-racist practice;
- seeking alliances which will promote anti-racist social work practice in local, national and international arenas;
- recognising the validity of anti-racist support groups for both black and white workers as legitimate workplace activities which take place during work time and require resourcing adequate for them to carry out their work;
- promoting the development of complaints procedures which can take effective action against those engaging in racist language and behaviour, including ensuring that these focus on an educational process whereby the accused is involved in understanding why such acts are offensive and unacceptable in a profession committed to respecting the dignity of both workers and 'clients' and operating within a social work framework.

Conclusion

In conclusion, anti-racist probation practice is about the creation of good practice which fosters the development of: more responsive and appropriate services for all 'clients' – black and white; egalitarian relationships in the workplace, and accountable, participative and democratic styles of management. Whilst anti-racist probation practice takes racial oppression within the Probation Service as its starting point for action, it must quickly move beyond the confines of its own organisational framework to encourage other parts of the criminal justice system to follow its example and to include within its remit dealing with other forms of oppression.

At the same time, anti-racist probation practice must focus on inputs, process and outcomes if the complexities of racism are to be unravelled. It must also address the multi-dimensionality of racism and tackle its presence at the personal, institutional and cultural levels if any changes which are secured are to endure over time.

Finally, by addressing all the fronts identified above, anti-racist probation practice will promote good practice for all workers and service users. Once these changes have been achieved and the Probation Service has succeeded in establishing the precondition for subsequent work, it can then turn its attention to creating a non-racist environment.

Our role in writing this book is to identify how progress towards such a goal can be achieved. Activating these suggestions depends on you as well as us. We hope you will take up our challenge and make your contribution to the creation of a non-oppressive criminal justice system.

Bibliography

Abernethy, R and Hammond, N (1992) *Drug Couriers: A Role for the Probation Service*. London: Middlesex Area Probation Service.

Ahmad, B (1990) *Black Perspectives in Social Work*. Birmingham: Venture Press.

Ahmad, WIU (ed.) (1993) *'Race' and Health In Contemporary Britain*. Buckingham: The Open University Press.

Ahmed, S (1991) 'Developing Anti-Racist Social Work Education Practice' in CCETSW/NCDP (eds), *Setting the Context for Change*. London: CCETSW.

Alfred, R (1992) *Black Workers in the Prison Service*. London: Prison Reform Trust.

Alibhai-Brown, Y (1988) 'Criminal Injustice' in *New Statesman and Society*, 8 July.

Alibhai-Brown, Y (1993) 'Social Workers Need Race Training Not Hysteria' in *The Independent*, 11 August.

Association of Chief Officers of Probation (ACOP) (1986) 'Report on Justice in a Multiracial Society'. Extract from *ACOP Conference Papers*, September.

Association of Chief Officers of Probation (1989) *Anti-Racism Policy Statement*. Wakefield: ACOP.

Association of Directors of Social Services (ADSS) (1978) *Multi-Racial Britain: The Social Services Response*. London: Commission for Racial Equality.

Avon Probation Service (APS) (1992) *Anti-Racism Strategy (2nd Draft)*. Avon: APS.

Baker, P, Hussain, Z and Saunders, J (1991) *Interpreters in Public Services*. Birmingham: Venture.

Barker, M (1981) *The New Racism: Conservatives and the Ideology of the Tribe*. London: Junction Books.

Bhat, A, Carr-Hill, R and Ohri, S (1988) *Britain's Black Population: A New Perspective*. Aldershot: Gower.

Bromley, C and Longino, CF, Jnr (1972) *White Racism and Black Americans.* Cambridge, Massachusetts: Schenkman.

Brooke, C (1993) 'Bottomley Promises Shake-up in Social Workers' Training' in *The Daily Mail,* 2 August, p. 5.

Brown, C (1984) *Black and White Britain: The Third Policy Studies Institute Survey.* London: Heinemann.

Browne, D (1990) *Black People, Mental Health and the Courts.* London: NACRO.

Browne, D (1993) 'Race Issues in Research on Psychiatry and Criminology' in Cook, D and Hudson, B (eds), *Racism and Criminology.* London: Sage.

Burgess, R (1993) 'Black Managers in the Probation Service'. MA dissertation, University of Bradford.

Burnett, R and Farrell, G (1994) *Reported and Unreported Racial Incidents in Prisons.* Centre for Criminological Research Occasional Paper No. 14. Oxford: Centre for Criminological Research.

Butler, T (1993) 'Race and the Staff of the Prison Service' in *Prison Report,* 22, Spring.

Campaign Against Double Punishment (CADP) (1992) *The Campaign Against Double Punishment.* Manchester: CADP.

Casale, S (1989) *Women Inside.* London: Civil Liberties Trust.

Cavadino, M and Dignan, J (1992) *The Penal System: An Introduction.* London: Sage.

Celnick, A (1993) 'Race and Rehabilitation' in Gelsthorpe, LR (ed.) *Minority Ethnic Groups in the Criminal Justice System.* Cropwood Conference Series No. 21. Cambridge: Institute of Criminology.

Central Council for Education and Training in Social Work (CCETSW) (1991). *Improving Standards in Practice Learning: Requirements and Guidance for the Approval of Agencies and the Accreditation and Training of Practice Teachers.* Paper 26.3. London: CCETSW.

Central Council for Education and Training in Social Work (1991a) *Requirements for the Diploma in Social Work.* Paper 30. London: CCETSW.

Central Council for Education and Training in Social Work/Northern Curriculum Development Project (CCETSW/NCDP) (eds) (1991) *Setting the Context for Change: Anti-Racist Social Work Education.* London: CCETSW.

Central Council of Probation Committees (CCPC) (1983) *Probation: A Multi-Racial Approach.* London: CCPC.

Central Council of Probation Committees (1986) *Discussion Paper on the Role of the Probation Service in the Inner Cities.* London: CCPC.

Central Council of Probation Committees (1987) *Black People and the Probation Service: Towards Racial Harmony.* London: CCPC.

Cervi, B and Clark, S (1993) 'Training Overhaul to Boost Public Image' in *Community Care,* 972:1, 24 June.

Cheney, D (1993) *Into the Dark Tunnel: Foreign Prisoners in the British Prison System*. London: Prison Reform Trust.

Cheney, D (1993a) 'Progress on Race Equality' in *Prison Report*, 23, Spring.

Cheney, D (1994) 'Policy and Practice in Work with Foreign Prisoners' in *Probation Journal*, 41(2), pp. 86–91.

Coard, B (1971) *How the West Indian Child is made Educationally Sub-normal in the British School System*. London: New Beacon Books.

Cohen, N (1994) 'Prejudiced Tories Attack Probation Rules' in *The Independent on Sunday*, 9 September.

Coleman, D (1988) *Coleman Review of Home Office Sponsorships*. London: Home Office.

Commission for Racial Equality (CRE) (1989) *Racial Equality in Social Services Departments: A Survey of Equal Opportunity Policies*. London: CRE.

Community Care (1993), 'Diploma Under Scrutiny in CCETSW Review' in *Community Care*, 980:2, 19 August.

Cook, D and Hudson, B (eds) (1993) *Racism and Criminology*. London: Sage.

Copes, R (1989) 'The Compulsory Detention of Afro-Caribbeans under the Mental Health Act' in *New Community*, April.

Criminal Justice Consultative Council (CJCC) (1991) *Race and the Criminal Justice System* quoted in NACRO, 1992.

Davies, M and Wright, R (1989) *Probation Training: A Consumer Perspective*. Norwich: University of East Anglia Monographs.

Davies, W and Ohri, A (1994) *An Approach to Equal Opportunity*. Sheffield: Organisation and Social Development Consultancy.

Day, M, Hall, T and Griffiths, C (1989) *Black People and the Criminal Justice System*. London: Howard League for Penal Reform.

Denney, D (1992) *Racism and Anti-Racism in Probation*. London: Routledge.

Denning, Lord (1982) *What Next in the Law?* London: Butterworth.

Dholakia, N (1994) 'Race and Equality: Black People and the Criminal Justice System' in *Criminal Justice Matters*, 16, Summer.

Dholakia, N and Sumner, M (1993) 'Research, Policy and Racial Justice' in Cook, D and Hudson, B (eds), *Racism and Criminology*. London: Sage.

Divine, D (1991) *Towards Real Communication: A Study of Confirmation Procedures in the West Midlands Probation Service*. London: CCETSW.

Divine, D (1991a) 'The Value of Anti-Racism in Social Work Education and Training' in CCETSW/NCDP (eds), *Setting the Context for Change*. London: CCETSW.

Dominelli, L (1983) *Women in Focus: Community Service Orders and Female Offenders*. Coventry: Warwick University.

Dominelli, L (1988) *Anti-Racist Social Work*. London: Macmillan (reprinted annually).

Dominelli, L (1989) 'An Uncaring Profession? An Examination of Racism in Social Work' in *New Community*, 15(3).

Dominelli, L (1992) 'Valuing Women' in Senior, P and Williams, B (eds), *Women, Values and Offending.* Sheffield: PAVIC Publications.

Dominelli, L (1993) 'Gender, Values and Offending: Where to Next?' in Senior, P and Williams, B (eds) *Gender and Offending.* Sheffield: PAVIC Publications.

Dominelli, L (1994) *Anti-Racist Social Work Education.* Paper presented at the 27th Congress of the International Association of the Schools of Social Work. Amsterdam, July.

Dominelli, L (1995) 'Deprofessionalising Social Work: Equal Opportunities, Anti-Oppressive Practice and Competencies' in *British Journal of Social Work.*

Dominelli, L, Patel, N and Thomas Bernard, W (1994) *Anti-Racist Social Work Education: Models for Practice.* Sheffield: Sheffield University.

Dunant, S (ed.) (1994) *The War of Words: The Political Correctness Debate.* London: Virago.

Durrant, J (1989) 'Continuous Agitation' in *Community Care*, 13 July, pp. 23–5.

Eaton, M (1993) *Women after Prison.* Buckingham: Open University Press.

Edwards, J (1990) 'What Purpose does Equality of Opportunity Serve?' in *New Community*, 17(2).

Eggleston, J (1986) *The Eggleston Report on the Education of Ethnic Minority Children in Britain.* Warwick University.

Eley, R (1989) 'Women and Management' in *Insight*, 14.

Ellis, S (1993) 'Equal Opportunities', Letter to the Editor, in *Prison Service Journal*, 90.

Faulkner, D (1985) *Probation Management in a Multiracial Society.* Paper presented to a Home Office Conference (quoted in NACRO, 1986, para. 4.18).

Fernando, S (1991) *Mental Health, Race and Culture.* London: Macmillan.

Fernando, S (1993) 'Combating Racism in Mental Health Services' in *Openmind*, 59:33–36, February–March.

Fielding, N and Fowles T (1991) 'Penal Policy File 41' in *Howard Journal*, 30(2).

Fishkin, J (1990) 'Equal Opportunities and Justice Between Generations' in *New Community*, 17(1), pp. 37–48.

Fletcher, H (1988) 'Black People and the Probation Service' in *NAPO News*, October.

Francis, J (1994) 'Last Among Equals' in *Community Care*, 13 January, pp. 14–15.

Fryer, P (1984) *Staying Power.* London: Pluto Press.

Genders, E and Player, E (1989) *Race Relations in Prisons.* Oxford: Clarendon.

Gibbon, P (1993) 'Equal Opportunities Policy and Race Equality' in Braham, P, Rattansi, A and Skellington, R (eds) *Racism and Anti-Racism: Inequalities, Opportunities and Policies.* London: Sage/Open University.

Gill, A and Marshall, T (1993) 'Working with Racist Offenders' in *Probation Journal*, 40(2), July.

Gilroy, P (1987) *There Ain't no Black in the Union Jack*. London: Hutchinson.

Glazer, N (1988) *The Limits of Social Policy*. London: Harvard University Press.

Gordon, P (1988) 'Black People and the Criminal Law: Rhetoric and Reality' in *International Journal of the Sociology of Law*, 16.

Gramsci, A (1971) *Selections from Prison Notebooks*. London: Lawrence and Wishart.

Green, R (1987) 'Racism and the Offender: A Probation Response' in Harding, J (ed.), *Probation and the Community*. London: Tavistock Publications.

Grimwood, GG (1994) *Personal Communication from the Equal Opportunities Manager, Personnel Planning Group*. London: Prison Service Headquarters, 19 October.

Hadjipavlou, S and Murphy, S (1991) *Report of a Scrutiny of Probation In-Service Training*. London: Home Office.

Hall, P, Land, H, Parker, R and Webb, A (1975) *Change, Choice and Conflict in Social Policy*. London: Heinemann.

Hall, S, Critcher, C, Jefferson, T, Clarke, J and Roberts, B (1978) *Policing the Crisis: Mugging, the State and Law and Order*. London: Macmillan.

Hall, T (1988) 'Race Relations and the Prison Service'. Public Lecture at the Prison Reform Trust. (Unpublished typescript.)

Hammersmith and Fulham Borough Council (1991) *Young People and the Criminal Justice System*. London: Hansib.

Hayles, M (1989) 'Promotion and Management: What Choice for Women' in *Probation Journal*, 17 March, p. 12.

Her Majesty's Chief Inspector of Prisons (HMCIP) (1990) *Annual Report*. London: HMCIP.

Her Majesty's Chief Inspector of Prisons (1992) *Annual Report*. London: HMCIP.

Her Majesty's Inspectorate of Probation (HMIP) (1993) *The Criminal Justice Act 1991 Inspection*. London: HMIP.

Her Majesty's Inspectorate of Probation (1993a) *Approved Probation and Bail Hostels*. London: HMIP.

Her Majesty's Inspectorate of Probation (1993b) *Offenders who Misuse Drugs: The Probation Service Response*. London: HMIP.

Her Majesty's Prison Service (HMPS) (1991) *Race Relations Manual*. London: Prison Service Directorate of Inmate Administration.

Her Majesty's Prison Service (1993) *Equal Opportunities in the Prison Service: Annual Progress Report*. London: Prison Service Personnel Management Division.

Her Majesty's Stationery Office (HMSO) (1976) *The 1976 Race Relations Act*. London: HMSO.

Her Majesty's Stationery Office (HMSO) (1992) *Race and the Criminal Justice System, CJA: Section 95*. London: Home Office.

Hercules, T (1989) *Labelled a Black Villain*. London: Fourth Estate.

Hill, M (1993) *New Agendas in the Study of the Policy Process*. London: Harvester Wheatsheaf.

Holdaway, S (1991) 'Probation in the Inner Cities: The Role of the Probation Committee'. Unpublished report to the Economic and Social Research Council. Sheffield: University of Sheffield Department of Sociological Studies.

Holdaway, S (1991a) *Recruiting a Multi-racial Police Force*. London: HMSO.

Holdaway, S and Allaker, J (1990) *Race Issues in the Probation Service: Review of Policy*. Wakefield: ACOP.

Holdaway, S and Mantle, G (1992) 'Governing the Probation Service: Probation Committees and Policy-making' in *Howard Journal*, 31(2).

Home Office (1977) *Probation and After-care Service – Ethnic Minorities*. Home Office Circular 113/1977. London: Home Office.

Home Office (1981) *Prison Department Circular Instructions*. Circular 28/1981. London: Home Office.

Home Office (1983) *Prison Department Circular Instructions*. Circular 56/ 1983. London: Home Office.

Home Office (1984) *Statement of National Objectives and Priorities for the Probation Service*. London: Home Office.

Home Office (1986) 'The Ethnic Origins of Prisoners'. *Statistical Bulletin*, 17/86. London: Home Office.

Home Office (1986a) *Prison Department Circular Instructions*. Circular 32/ 1986. London: Home Office.

Home Office (1988) *Probation Service Policies on Race*. Circular No. 75/88. London: Home Office, C6 Division.

Home Office (1991) *Discussion Document: Towards National Standards for Pre-Sentence Reports*. London: Home Office.

Home Office (1991a) *Organising Supervision and Punishment in the Community*. London: Home Office.

Home Office (1992) *Race and the Criminal Justice System*. London: Home Office.

Home Office (1992a) *Criminal Statistics for England and Wales*. London: Home Office.

Home Office (1994) *National Framework for the Throughcare of Offenders in Custody to the Completion of Supervision in the Community*. London: Home Office.

Home Office Research and Statistics Department (HORSD) (1993) 'Ethnic Origins of Probation Staff 1992' in *Home Office Statistical Bulletin* 27/93. London: Home Office.

Home Office Research and Statistics Department (1994) 'The Ethnic Origins of Prisoners' in *Home Office Statistical Bulletin* 21/94. London: Home Office.

Hood, R (1992) *A Question of Judgement: Race and Sentencing*. London: Commission for Racial Equality.

Hood, R (1992a) *Race and Sentencing*, Oxford: Clarendon Press.

hooks, b (1992) *Sisters of the Yam: Black Women and Self-Recovery*. Toronto: Between the Lines.

hooks, b (1993) *Black Looks: Black Representation in the Media*. London: Southend Press.

Hudson, B (1989) 'Discrimination and Disparity: The Influence of Race on Sentencing' in *New Community*, 16(1), pp. 23–34.

Hudson, B (1993) 'Penal Policy and Racial Justice' in Gelsthorpe, LR (ed.), *Minority Ethnic Groups in the Criminal Justice System*. Cropwood Conference Series No. 21. Cambridge: University of Cambridge Institute of Criminology.

Hudson, B (1993a) 'Racism and Criminology: Concepts and Controversies' in Cook, D and Hudson, B (eds), *Racism and Criminology*. London: Sage.

Husband, C (1991) 'Race, Conflictual Politics, and Anti-Racist Social Work: Lessons from the Past for Action in the 90s' in CCETSW/NCDP (eds), *Setting the Context for Change*. London: CCETSW.

Inner London Probation Service (ILPS) (1993) *Anti-Racist Training Pack*. London: ILPS.

Jacobs, J and Grear, M (1977) 'Drop Outs and Rejects: An Analysis of the Prison Guard's Revolving Door' in *Criminal Justice Review*, 2(2).

James, M (1992) 'A Duty not to Discriminate – What Might This Mean for Probation Practice?' in Williams, B and Senior, P (eds), *Probation Practice after the Criminal Justice Act 1991*. Sheffield: PAVIC Publications.

Jeevanjee, A (1993) 'Prisons – Privatisation – Racism'. Letter to the Editor in *Prison Service Journal*, 90.

Jewson, N and Mason, D (1993) 'The Theory and Practice of Equal Opportunities Policies: Liberal and Radical Approaches' in Braham, P, Rattansi, A and Skellington, R (eds), *Racism and Anti-Racism: Inequalities, Opportunities and Policies*. London: Sage.

Kay, S (1993) 'Judgements of Worth' in *Probation Journal*, 40(2).

Kelly, L (1988) *Surviving Sexual Violence*. Cambridge: Polity Press.

Kennedy, H (1992) *Eve was Framed*. London: Macmillan.

Kett, J, Collett, S, Barron, C, Hill, I and Metherell, D (1992) *Managing and Developing Anti-Racist Practice within Probation: A Resource Pack for Action*. St Helens: Merseyside Probation Service.

King, A (1993) 'The Impact of Incarceration on African American Families: Implications for Practice' in *Families in Society*, 74, March.

King, J (1993) 'When Love is Not Enough' in *Community Care*, 979: 18–19, 12 August.

King, M and May, C (1985) *Black Magistrates*. London: The Cobden Trust.

Lorde, A (1984) *Sister Outsider*. New York: The Crossing Press.

Luthra, M and Oakley, R (1991) *Combatting Racism through Training*. Centre of Research in Ethnic Relations, University of Warwick.

Maden, A, Swinton, M and Gunn, J (1992) 'The Ethnic Origin of Women Serving a Prison Sentence' in *British Journal of Criminology*, 32(2).

Mann, CR (1993) *Unequal Justice: A Question of Color*. Bloomington, Indiana: Indiana University Press.

Mason, M (1992) 'Disability Equality in the Classroom: A Human Rights Issue' in Reiser, D and Mason, M (eds), *Disability Equality in Education*. London: Independent Publication.

Mavunga, P (1993) 'Probation: A Basically Racist Service' in Gelsthorpe, LR (ed.), *Minority Ethnic Groups in the Criminal Justice System*. Cropwood Conference Series No. 21. Cambridge: University of Cambridge Institute of Criminology.

Mayhew, R and May, C (1993) *The British Crime Survey*. London: Home Office.

McDermott, K (1990) 'We Have No Problem: The Experience of Racism in Prison' in *New Community*, 16(2), January.

McLeod, E (1982) *Women Working: Prostitution Now*. London: Croom Helm.

Middlesex Area Probation Service (MAPS) (1991) *Corporate Strategy 1991–1994: Race Issues*. London: MAPS.

Mills, H (1993) 'Swastika Displayed by Prison Officers in Reception Area' in *The Independent*, 15 November.

Morris, A (1987) *Women, Crime and the Criminal Justice System*. Oxford: Basil Blackwell.

Morris, J (1991) *Women and Disability*. Harmondsworth: Penguin.

Morris, L (1994) *Dangerous Classes: The Underclass and Social Citizenship*. Routledge.

Morris, P (1989) 'Foot in the Door for a Racial Perspective' in *Community Care*, Free Supplement, 26 October, pp. iv–v.

Murray, C (1984) *Losing Ground: American Social Policy, 1950–1980*. New York: Basic Books.

National Association for the Care and Resettlement of Offenders (NACRO) (1986) *Black People and the Criminal Justice System*. London: NACRO.

National Association for the Care and Resettlement of Offenders (1991) *Black Communities and the Probation Service: Working Together. Report of a Sub-Committee of the NACRO Race Issues Advisory Committee*. London: NACRO.

National Association for the Care and Resettlement of Offenders (1991a) *Black People's Experience of Criminal Justice*. London: NACRO.

National Association for the Care and Resettlement of Offenders (1991b) 'Race and Criminal Justice' in *NACRO Briefing*. London: NACRO.

National Association for the Care and Resettlement of Offenders (1992) *Black People Working in the Criminal Justice System*. London: NACRO.

National Association for the Care and Resettlement of Offenders (1992a) *Race Policies into Action, the Implementation of Equal Opportunities Policies in Criminal Justice Agencies. Report of the NACRO Race Issues Advisory Committee.* London: NACRO.

National Association for the Care and Resettlement of Offenders (1992b) 'Statistics on Black People Working in the Criminal Justice System' in *NACRO Briefing*, 109, London: NACRO.

National Association for the Care and Resettlement of Offenders (1993) *NACRO Briefing*, 32, London: NACRO.

National Association for the Care and Resettlement of Offenders (1993a) *Race and Criminal Justice: Training. Report of the Race Issues Advisory Committee.* London: NACRO.

National Association for the Care and Resettlement of Offenders (1993b) 'Summary of Her Majesty's Chief Inspector's Report on Her Majesty's Prison, Leicester' in *NACRO Criminal Justice Digest*, 75, January.

National Association for the Care and Resettlement of Offenders (1994) *NACRO Criminal Justice Digest*, 79, January.

National Association of Probation Officers (NAPO) (1985) *NAPO and Racism.* NEC 47/85. London: NAPO.

National Association of Probation Officers (1987) *Access to Justice: Proceedings of a Professional Conference.* London: NAPO.

National Association of Probation Officers (1989) 'Black Probation Staff' (news item) in *NAPO News*, September.

National Association of Probation Officers (1991) *Developing an Anti-racist Probation Practice: NAPO's Manifesto for Action* (2nd edn). London: NAPO.

National Association for Probation Officers, West Yorkshire Branch (NAPOWYPSB) (1987) *Racism and Probation.* Ilkley: Owen Wells.

Nixon, J (1980) 'The Importance of Communication in the Implementation of Government Policy at Local Level' in *Policy and Politics*, 8(2).

Nixon, J (1984) 'Race Relations Policy: The Role of the Home Office' in Lewis, D and Wallace, H (eds), *Policies into Practice: National and International Case Studies in Implementation.* London: Heinemann.

Office of Population Censuses and Surveys (OPCS) (1985) *Staff Attitudes in the Prison Service.* London: HMSO.

Ohri, A (1988) *Model for Developing and Assessing Anti-Racist Practice.* Sheffield: Ohri Associates.

Ohri, A (1991) *Face of Diversity: The Black Voluntary Sector in West Yorkshire.* Sheffield: Organisation and Social Development Policy.

Oliver, M (1990) *The Politics of Disablement.* London: Macmillan.

Patel, N (1991) 'The Curriculum Development Project: Model and Process, 1988–1990' in CCETSW/NCDP (eds), *Setting the Context for Change.* London: CCETSW.

Patel, N (1994) *Establishing a Framework for Anti-Racist Social Work Education in a Multi-Racial Society: The UK Experience from a Statutory Body*. Paper presented at the 27th Congress of the International Association of Schools of Social Work. Amsterdam, July.

Peelo, M, Stewart, J, Stewart, G and Prior, A (1991) 'Women Partners of Prisoners' in *Howard Journal*, 30(4).

Phillips, M (1993) 'An Oppressive Urge to End Oppression' in *The Observer*, 1 August.

Pinker, R (1993) 'A Lethal Kind of Looniness' in *The Times Higher Educational Supplement*, 10 September, p. 19.

Powell, D and Edmonds, J (1985) 'Are You Racist Too?' in *Community Care*, 14 September.

Prashar, U (1987) 'Too much Talk and Not Enough Positive Action' in Benyon, J and Solomos, J (eds), *The Roots of Urban Unrest*. Oxford: Pergamon.

Priestley, P (1972) 'The Prison Welfare Officer: The Case of Role Strain' in *British Journal of Sociology*, 23(2), pp. 221–35.

Prison Reform Trust (1991) *The Woolf Report: A Summary of the Main Findings and Recommendations of the Inquiry into Prison Disturbances*. London: Prison Reform Trust.

Raban, T (1987) 'Removed from the Community: Prisoners and the Probation Service' in Harding, J (ed.), *Probation and the Community*. London: Tavistock.

Rattansi, A (1992) 'Changing the Subject? Racism, Culture and Education' in Donald, J and Rattansi, A (eds), *'Race', Culture and Difference*. Milton Keynes: Open University Press, pp. 11–48.

Raynor, P, Roberts, S, Thomas, L and Vanstone, M (1994). *Confirming Probation Officers in Appointment*. Sheffield: PAVIC Publications. (Also summarised in *Probation Journal*, December.)

Reardon, B (1993) 'The Reality of Life for Black Professionals in the Criminal Justice System' in Senior, P and Woodhill, D (eds), *Justice for Black Young People*. Sheffield: PAVIC Publications.

Ridley, J (1980) 'Implications of Rastafarianism amongst Young West Indians in Slough'. BA dissertation, University of Reading.

Rooney, B (1982) 'Black Social Workers in White Departments' in Cheetham, J (ed.), *Social Work and Ethnicity*. Hemel Hempstead: George Allen and Unwin.

Ross, R (1990) *Time to Think: A Cognitive Model of Offender Rehabilitation and Delinquency Prevention. Research Summary*. The Cognitive Centre Foundation, University of Ottawa.

Rushdie, S (1982) 'The New Empire within Britain' in *New Society*, 9 December, pp. 417–20.

Sashidharan, SP (1986) 'The Politics and Ideology of Transcultural

Psychiatry' in Cox, JL (ed.), *Transcultural Psychiatry*. London: Croom Helm.

Scarman, Lord (1981) *The Brixton Disorders 10–12 April 1981: Report of an Inquiry*. London: HMSO.

Schofield, H (1994) 'Withdrawal from Prisons' in *NAPO News*, 62, July/August.

Shallice, A and Gordon, P (1990) *Black People, White Justice? Race and the Criminal Justice System*. London: Runnymede Trust.

Shaw, S (1993) 'Race Issues: Brickbats and Bouquets?' in *Prison Report*, 22, Spring.

Shaw, S (1994) 'Action for Race Equality' in *Prison Report*, 28, Autumn.

Sibeon, R (1991) *Towards a New Sociology of Social Work*. Aldershot: Avebury.

Sim, J (1994) 'Reforming the Penal Wasteland: A Critical Review of the Woolf Report', in Player, E and Jenkins, M (eds), *Prisons after Woolf: Reform through Riot*. London: Routledge.

Sivanandan, A (1985) 'RAT and the Degradation of Black Struggle' in *Race and Class*, 26(4).

Sivanandan, A (1992) *Deadly Silence: Deaths in Custody*. London: Institute of Race Relations.

Skellington, R and Morris, P (1992) *Race in Britain Today*. London: Sage.

Smellie, E and Crow, I (1991) *Black People's Experience of the Criminal Justice System*. London: NACRO.

Smith, D (1976) *The Facts of Racial Disadvantage. The Third Policy Studies Institute Report*. Harmondsworth: Penguin.

Smith, DJ (1994) 'Race, Crime and Criminal Justice' in Maguire, M, Morgan, R and Reiner, R (eds), *Oxford Handbook of Criminology*. Oxford: Clarendon Press.

South Yorkshire Probation Service (SYPS) (1993) *Probation, Race and Anti-Racism*. Sheffield: SYPS.

South Yorkshire Probation Service (undated) *Anti-Racist Policy Document*. Sheffield: SYPS.

Sparks, R (1994) 'Can Prisons be Legitimate?' in *British Journal of Criminology*, Special Issue, 34, pp. 14–28.

Spencer, J (1993) 'Criminal Justice and the Politics of Scrutiny' in *Social Policy and Administration*, 27(1), March.

Stone, I (1988) *Equal Opportunities in Local Authorities: Developing Effective Strategies of the Implementation of Policies for Women*. London: HMSO.

Swann, L (1985) *Education for All: The Report of the Committee of Enquiry into the Education of Children from Ethnic Minority Groups*. Cmnd 9453. London: HMSO.

Tarzi, A and Hedges, J (1990) *A Prison Within A Prison: A Study of Foreign Prisoners*. London: Inner London Probation Service.

Taylor, W (1981) *Probation and After-Care in a Multi-Racial Society*. London: Commission for Racial Equality.

Thompson, N (1994) *Anti-Discriminatory Practice*. London: BASW/Macmillan.

Tonkin, B (1987) 'State of the Art' in *Community Care*, 12 March.

Towl, G (1993) 'Groupwork in Prisons' in *Probation Journal*, 40(4), pp. 208–9.

Voakes, R and Fowler, Q (1989) *Sentencing, Race and Social Enquiry Reports*. Wakefield: West Yorkshire Probation Service.

Ward, I (1994) 'Retention of Prison Officers from Ethnic Minorities'. Letter to the Editor in *Prison Service Journal*, 93.

Webb, T and Liff, S (1988) 'Play the White Man: The Social Construction of Fairness and Competition in Equal Opportunity Policies' in *Sociological Review*, 38(3).

West Midlands Probation Service (WMPS) (1986) *Not Back to Normal: A Report to the WMPS Following Lozells and Handsworth Disturbances of September 1985*. Birmingham: WMPS.

West Yorkshire Police (1991) *Juvenile Offending Record*. Wakefield: West Yorkshire Police.

West Yorkshire Probation Service (WYPS) (1994) *Anti-Racism Policy and Codes of Practice*. Green Circular 3/94. Wakefield: WYPS.

Whitehouse, P (1978) 'Ethnic Minorities' in *West Midlands Probation and Aftercare Service Bulletin*, July.

Whitehouse, P (1980) *Probation in a Multi-Racial Context*. Paper presented to the British Psychological Society Conference. Bradford University, 22–28, March.

Whitehouse, P (1983) 'Race, Bias and Social Enquiry Reports' in *Probation Journal*, 30(2).

Whitehouse, P (1986) 'Race and the Criminal Justice System' in Coombe, V and Little, A (eds), *Race and Social Work: A Guide to Training*. London: Tavistock.

Williams, B (1991) *Work with Prisoners*. Birmingham: Venture Press.

Williams, B (1992) 'Caring Professionals or Street-Level Bureaucrats? The Case of Probation Officers' Work with Prisoners' in *Howard Journal*, 31(4).

Williams, B (1995) 'Towards Justice in Probation Work with Prisoners' in Ward, D and Lacey, M (eds), *Probation: Working for Justice*. London: Whiting and Birch.

Wilson, A (1977) *Finding a Voice*. London: Virago.

Woolf, Lord Justice (1991) *Prison Disturbances, April 1990, Cm 1456*. London: HMSO.

Worrall, A (1990) *Offending Women: Female Lawbreakers and the Criminal Justice System*. London: Routledge.

Worrall, A (1994) *'Have you got a Minute?': The Changing Role of Prison Boards of Visitors*. London: Prison Reform Trust.

Zamble, E and Porporino, FJ (1988) *Coping Behavior and Adaptation in Prison Inmates*. New York: Springer-Verlag.

Name index

Subject index